Testimonials

"I couldn't put it down! I was up until 5:15 this morning finishing it. The imagery you used pulled me in and made it all so REAL. I pray your story reaches far and wide for the glory of God. You have done well, a good and faithful servant."

—Yavonna H

"I read it ALL today. What a testament of God's faithfulness! You did a wonderful job giving God the glory at every turn, and weaving His grace and provision in each chapter."

—Sarah E

"Well, I couldn't put it down & finished it already! No words! Definitely many tears, some giggles, and so much that I can relate to, and I know SO many others will as well! What a wild but BEAUTIFUL testimony! This is gonna do big things!"

—Stephanie B

"I read the first 5 chapters yesterday. Wow. It's compelling and easy to read. It draws the readers in and keeps them wanting to know more. Well done, good and faithful servant."

—Terri P

"I heard you give a little bit of your testimony at the ladies event a while back. But reading it and all the little details, wow! You have such a testimony, and God is using you to speak truth to so many!"

—Holly T

MUSLIM BY BIRTH

CHRISTIAN BY CHOICE

Muslim by Birth
Christian by Choice

*Discovering Personal Truth
and Identity in Christ*

Karima Burdette

Copyright © 2025 Karima Burdette, *First Edition*.

All Rights Reserved. No portion of this book may be reproduced, stored in a retrieval system, or transmitted in any form or by any means – electronic, mechanical, photocopy, recording, scanning, or other – except for brief quotations in critical reviews or articles, without the prior written permission of the author.

Unless otherwise noted, scripture quotations are taken from the Holy Bible, New International Version, NIV, Copyright ©1973, 1978, 1984, 2011 by Biblica, Inc. Used by permission of Zondervan. All rights reserved worldwide. www.zondervan.com. The "NIV" and "New International Version" are trademarks registered in the United States Patent and Trademark Office by Biblica, Inc.

Scripture quotations noted as (ESV) are from the ESV Bible (The Holy Bible, English Standard Version), © 2001 by Crossway, a publishing ministry of Good News Publishers. Used by permission. All rights reserved. The ESV text may not be quoted in any publication made available to the public by a Creative Commons license. The ESV may not be translated in whole or in part into any other language.

Fonts and stock images licensed for commercial use.

Author: Burdette, Karima
Title: Muslim by Birth, Christian by Choice: Discovering Personal Truth and Identity in Christ
Hardcover ISBN: 979-8-9986458-0-8
Softcover ISBN: 979-8-9986458-1-5
eBook ISBN: 979-8-9986458-2-2
Audio ISBN: 979-8-9986458-3-9
Library of Congress Control Number: 2025908032
Cover Design: Viyanca
Book Design: Russ Davis, Bravo Book Design

Printed in the United State of America.

Note from the Author

As I sit down to write this, I am humbled and awed that God has brought me this far. I wouldn't be here without Him, and I am so grateful for the ability to look back on my life and see all the ways He has worked. I pray that this book would encourage you to look back over your own life—I promise you won't have to search long before you can see His faithful hand in your own story.

I would like to make it clear that I am no Bible scholar, just a woman who has been changed by the blood of Jesus Christ and saved by His grace. Nothing good you will see about me is from me—it is all Him.

This is my personal story, and I am not judging anyone based on their religion. I believe that your religion is your personal choice. The purpose of this book is to simply walk you through my trials and victories, and show you where the hope is that I have found.

That hope in my life is Jesus. I believe that as much as your family loves you, they cannot save you. The only one who can intercede for us and give salvation is Jesus Christ. He died on the cross for our sins, and three days later rose from the dead, showing His power over sin and death.

No matter where you are in life or what struggles you are experiencing, just know that you are not alone. You have a

Father in heaven Who loves you and accepts you, and is waiting with open arms to receive you into His family.

Because of my salvation, I am overwhelmed with joy and gratitude, and want to share it with the world. After years of searching for love, identity and purpose in all the wrong places, I found Jesus, and He has set me free from the guilt and shame I once felt. I am just so thankful for all He has done for me.

I pray that this book will encourage and inspire you. Regardless of where you are in your faith, I pray that through my story, you can see that God can radically transform your life if you let Him in.

Acknowledgements

I want to sincerely express my deep gratitude to my Lord Jesus Christ for saving me. I wouldn't be here today or have written this book without His unfailing love and grace towards me. I am deeply thankful for the love of my life, my sweet husband, Roger, along with my children, Zecharia and Priscilla, for their unwavering love and support. You are my inspiration and my heart.

To my parents—I cannot thank you enough for your sacrifices for me throughout my life. You always encouraged me to chase my dreams, and I wouldn't have made it this far without you. I would also like to acknowledge my younger sisters and their families for their encouragement, support and affection.

I also wish to recognize my other family and friends in the U.S., France, Morocco, and Spain for their love, motivation and help in writing this book. Additionally, I am thankful for my church, Compassion Christian Church, and to all of my pastors for their inspiration, especially Pastor Cam.

I want to extend my appreciation to my dear friend, Elisa, for connecting me with Becky and Tori—I truly couldn't have completed this book without the three of you. God undeniably brought our wonderful team together, and you all have been fantastic.

Finally, I would also like to thank my graphic designer, Viyanca, and my photographer, Casey, for their exceptional work on this project.

Love you all! And may Jesus be glorified through it all.

—Karima Burdette

Note: All persons within are actual individuals; there are no composite characters. The names of some individuals have been changed to respect their privacy.

Contents

1. The Colonel 1
2. Generational Scars 6
3. Christmas in July 12
4. A Faraway God 18
5. Free at Last 27
6. Late Bloomer 36
7. American Dreaming 47
8. Finding Myself, Losing Myself 54
9. When Dreams Go Dark 62
10. Sworn to Silence 67
11. A Tiny Little Thing 75
12. Resident Alien 80
13. Gone for Good 89
14. Moroccan Redneck 95
15. Blue Eyes and Biceps 102
16. Rebirth 110
17. Superman 116
18. Growing Roots 128
19. Surrender 136
20. Growing a Family, Growing in Faith 144
21. The Silent Rupture 162

22. Transforming Grace.. 169
23. Runaway Heart 177
24. When Faith is All That Remains........................ 183

Invitation 209
About the Author.. 210
Endnote Review Request... 211

Muslim by Birth
Christian by Choice

Chapter 1

The Colonel

"Before I formed you in the womb I knew you, before you were born I set you apart; I appointed you as a prophet to the nations." —Jeremiah 1:5

I was 2 years old when my mother brought me to live with my grandparents

"Get up!"

I tried to force my eyes open. I could feel my fellow soldiers' sweaty bodies pressing close to mine under the shared, scratchy blanket. My body yearned for just a few more minutes of sleep.

"Get up!"

The Colonel was in a worse mood than usual. I opened my eyes just in time to see a foot hurtling past my face toward my ribs. I braced for impact. *Thud!*

"GET UP!"

We scrambled to our feet. It was 4 a.m.—a new day, a new mission, and if we didn't complete it successfully, we'd be beaten. Every night, that stern voice echoed in my dreams—more like my nightmares.

You see, the Colonel was no ordinary person. That was the nickname we gave to my grandmother—my fellow soldiers and I, who were actually my aunts.

Growing up in the crowded city of Marrakech, Morocco, our "missions" were pretty simple—my aunts and I were tasked with stealing food. After the famous morning kicks to get us up and going, my three aunts and I headed out into the shadowed streets. I remember how terrifying those mornings were, walking to the marketplace in the eerie darkness. The only people out at that hour were up to no good, so we would press our little bodies close together, linking arms as we walked. When I was especially tired, I would close my eyes, thinking I would somehow get more rest as I walked.

Once we got to the bustling market, we worked as a team, with my two older aunts distracting the merchants so that my youngest aunt and I could snatch as much food as possible. It worked without fail, but I was always scared of being caught and getting in trouble or being beaten by the salespeople. However, I was even more scared of the beating I would get at home if my bag wasn't full—that was the thought motivating all of us to succeed.

After we had stolen enough, we headed home for a breakfast of soup and dates, and then I would walk to school. When I was younger, my school was only a half mile from our home and either my grandmother or one of my aunts would walk me there since I was so little. When I was around eight years old and went to a different school, I walked alone, two miles each way.

I would come home for lunch because most places in Morocco, including the schools, would close from 12 p.m. to 2 p.m. for lunch. My afternoon duties consisted of heading to the *souk*, or shopping area, with my youngest aunt to beg tourists for money before heading back to school for a few more hours. After school got out in the evening, I would be back out stealing with one of my older aunts until dinner.

Being a little girl worked for me—I was a pretty good beggar. My aunt and I would work up our courage as we approached groups of tourists, who could often be cruel. I always had better luck approaching the women, and with our sad eyes, big smiles and ragged clothes, we did okay.

"Hi, ma'am, can you please help us? We are hungry," I'd say.

Normally, they would ask my name.

"My name is Karima. Can you please give us some money so that we can eat today?" My aunt would chime in, "Yes, please help us, we don't have any food."

If I was given any money, I gave it to my aunt to hold and we moved on to the next tourist and did it all over again. Sometimes, we would use a little of the money we made begging to buy cheap souvenirs, and then try to resell those to tourists for a profit. I remember buying these handmade headbands that we gave the lady tourists as a "gift," and most times they would give us something in return. We always kept some of the money, so that if we ever had a bad day begging we still had something to give my grandmother to hopefully avoid a beating.

The souk never closed and was always full of people selling all sorts of handmade goods, like rugs, ceramics, wooden items, jewelry, and clothes. Marrakech has always been a popular vacation spot, so there was no lack of wealthy Europeans, Asians and Americans wandering around. One of my clearest memories from the years I lived there was watching the different tourist couples. I would watch the man and how he cared for his wife, and a deep part of my soul yearned for that kind of connection and love. My dream as a little girl was to grow up and marry a foreigner from overseas and have two children of my own, a boy and a girl.

Most of the tourists ignored us, spit on us, or called us names. Some were even afraid to come near us for fear we carried diseases. Since tourism is the main industry for Morocco's economy, the souk was full of cops, even undercover cops, who were there to "protect" the tourists from beggars like me. On one occasion, I was talking to some tourists when an undercover cop snuck up behind me and kicked me hard in my private area. I was just a little child at the time, but I remember bleeding, and the pain being so bad I could barely walk.

Every once in a while, someone kind and generous would give us candy or money. One French lady took me and my aunt and our friend to a bakery and bought us whatever we wanted. This was such a special treat for us, because normally if we bought any pastries with a little of the money we made, they were old or expired.

We used to buy these little cream-filled pastries that were a few days old, and when we got them the cream was always yellow and sour. We didn't care—it was food. She also gave us money and took a picture with us and gave it to us. I still have that picture to this day—I would love to thank her now if I could. She could never have known what her small act of kindness to that little girl all those years ago meant to me.

Those few fond memories are like little rays of sunshine in my very dark childhood. I hated all the lying and stealing and begging, but I had to do it to survive living with my grandmother. Living in constant fear of her for those ten years set the tone of my life for many years to come, setting me on a search for any sense of belonging. I never felt I was good enough for my grandmother—to the day she died, she treated everyone in her life with harshness and criticism. I wouldn't find out until much later in life why she was so miserable—all I knew was that she made *my* life miserable.

I remember how my heart raced when I heard the familiar padding of her sandals in the hallway. I remember the names she called me, all the times she cussed me out. I remember her yelling at me and my aunts and uncles for talking, playing or laughing. I remember all the times I quickly put on any extra clothes I had in preparation for being beaten with palm branches. I remember the kicks, the screaming, the crying. I remember the emptiness. I remember the fear. I remember the hopelessness. But most of all, I remember feeling like I didn't belong.

Chapter 2

Generational Scars

For he chose us in him before the creation of the world to be holy and blameless in his sight. In love he predestined us for adoption to sonship through Jesus Christ, in accordance with his pleasure and will… —Ephesians 1:4-5

My grandmother was a petite woman, about 5'1". She was beautiful, fierce and a hard worker—and she was always busy. She had to be to survive her life. Her parents married her off to my grandfather when she was only fourteen years old. He was such a kind man, but at least ten years her senior. They were both uneducated and never made a good income—he ran a fruit stand and she took care of the home and the children. Although it was cheap to live in Morocco, it was difficult to make a living if you were uneducated.

Together they had fourteen children, eight of whom lived to adulthood. Two of their babies were stillborn, and another four died shortly after birth due to different illnesses. My mother was one of her older children, which is how I was close in age to my mom's younger brothers and sisters, the aunts and uncles I grew up with.

The quality I remember most about my grandmother is her cruelty–it was as if she wanted to take out her bitterness over her lost childhood on every person in her life. She was physically and verbally abusive toward all her children, grandchildren, and husband. All of us were terrified of her. I remember getting beatings from her, running from her and hiding behind one of my aunts when she came at me with a palm branch stick. I would cry and beg, screaming, "Please don't hit me! Don't hit me, Grandma!" She always got to me despite my desperate pleas for mercy.

One of my aunts recalled a memory from before I was born, when she was about four or five years old living at my grandmother's house and dealing with her abuse. She said there was one day where she was almost kidnapped as a child—she was playing outside, and a stranger tried to walk off with her. Thankfully, my grandfather came home from work at the same time and brought her back before they got too far away. When he brought her inside and confronted my grandmother about what happened, instead of being upset that her daughter was almost taken, my grandmother gave my aunt a beating. It was bad enough that my aunt remembers to this day—she said she was hit so hard on the neck that she was bleeding.

The abuse had far-reaching effects into the future for all of us who were raised in that house. My grandmother could never have realized at the time. When you grow up believing you'll never measure up to your parent's standard, you are willing to accept less from others. My mother was a prime example of that.

Looking for love and acceptance in the wrong places, she married my father when she was about seventeen (we don't know exactly how old she was since neither she nor her siblings had birth certificates). Unlike most marriages at the time, it was not arranged by the woman's parents; my parents met through a mutual friend, and they were very much in love.

After a few years of marriage, it became apparent that my dad was no better than my grandmother, as he became physically abusive toward my mom. Like many women going through domestic violence, she gave him second and third and fourth chances, forgiving him many times and hoping that somehow he would change. She even tried to get away a couple of times when I was a little baby. She made it all the way to the train station before he caught up with her and forced her to come back home with him.

It wasn't until I was about two years old that my mom got up the courage to ask him for a divorce. Her breaking point happened when my grandmother and some of her siblings came to visit her and my dad. While they were there, my dad started insulting my mom right in front of them. That night, she returned home to Marrakech with her family and started the divorce process.

Still young, and at that point terrified, she knew she couldn't take care of me and support us both on her own. She had never been to school, so she couldn't read or write. Although there was free public school in Morocco at the time, it was optional, and the government didn't oversee kids going to school like it does in the U.S. In 1976, when I was about two years old, she made one of the hardest decisions a parent can make—giving up her own child.

My grandparents took me in, and she was able to get a job as a nanny so that she could send school supplies and money to support me, as well as money to support my grandparents and her siblings. It was very important to her that I went to school, since she didn't get that opportunity. I am so grateful for that desire of hers, as it wasn't the norm back then for kids to go to school. My mom thought my grandmother would treat me kindly, as the first grandchild and youngest in the house. That, of course, was far from what happened.

For the ten years between 1976 to 1986, I lived in Marrakech, Morocco with my grandparents. My mom moved back to the city of Mohammedia, over two hours away, where my dad was from and where I was born. She worked there so she could send money back for us.

My dad visited me one time, when I was around four or five years old. I don't remember much; there is one picture of us from his visit, and I don't look happy. I'm sure I was uncomfortable since I didn't know him at all. All I remember is going to the *Jemaa el Fna* square to walk around with him and my mom, who was only there to protect me.

In 1981, my mom met my stepdad through a friend of a friend while he was in Mohammedia on business. They told me it was love at first sight, and when my stepdad had to move back home to France two months later, he asked my mom to marry him. At the time, I wasn't able to join them—his job had him traveling constantly. I think my mom was also scared to take me from my grandmother, who enjoyed the financial support she was receiving from my mom. There definitely was a benefit to her keeping me around.

Those ten years in Morocco, from age two to twelve, I grew up with two of my uncles and three of my aunts, who were more like siblings since we were so close in age and were going through the same abuse at the hands of my grandmother. We laughed together and cried together, told jokes and danced together (those few times we were able to fly under my grandmother's fun-hating radar).

We didn't have any toys, but we made up our own games and used our imaginations. Our favorite part of the day was early afternoon, the hottest part of the day, when my grandmother took a nap. All of us kids would gather in a room and talk about our day and commiserate, but mostly we tried to talk about happy things to take our minds off of our lives for a minute. We loved when my grandmother had visitors to the house—if we were lucky, they stayed for a few hours and occupied her time. She never paid attention to us when there were other people around, so those times were precious to all of us.

I always called my grandfather *abba*, or father, and her *moue*, or mother, along with my aunts and uncles, since I was treated just as terribly as all her other children. She treated strangers better than us; she treated strangers like they were her own kids. She would give them food, money we stole, gifts my mom had sent for us. At the holidays, she would even give money to the poor. She craved importance and respect and to be *somebody* so much that she made all of us nobodies.

I remember my mom sent me this little doll as a gift, and as my grandmother opened the box and pulled it out, I was so excited to finally be getting a toy that I could play with. After that day when it came in the mail, I never saw it again—it sat in my grandmother's room until the day she died.

The Colonel told us what to do and when to do it; we couldn't do anything on our own, and that is not an exaggeration. Even as adults, my aunts and uncles and even my mom still allowed her to control their comings and goings and everything they did when they visited her.

I was known to my grandmother as "the daughter of the crazy man." I missed my mother so badly, but was too afraid to tell her what was going on. Since my grandmother's abuse was all I really knew, I thought it was normal, my situation was hopeless, and that not even my mom would be able to help me get out of it.

Chapter 3

Christmas in July

Shout for joy, you heavens; rejoice, you earth; burst into song, you mountains! For the Lord comforts his people and will have compassion on his afflicted ones. —Isaiah 49:13

A small piece of my heart will always belong to Morocco. It is a country full of amazing people who are kind, hospitable and cheerful. If I close my eyes, I can almost feel the hot, dry air heavy in my lungs, smell the freshly baked pastries and hear the merchants hawking their wares. The sharp scent of spiced lamb cuts through, and I can feel the bustle of tourists, entertainers, snake charmers, beggars and pedestrians—I'm back in the souk, darting past booths with my aunts, trying to steal enough food to avoid my grandmother's rage.

Summers in Marrakech were almost unbearable, with temperatures in the triple digits most days. I slept on the tile floor with my aunts, squished together under one blanket like sardines. I can vividly remember pressing up against the wall because the tiles were cool on my bare tummy.

My aunts would take off their *jalabas*, or robes, on those hot summer nights and hang them in our doorway. They looked like shadowy people at night, which scared me. I never had to wear one because I was so little, but my aunts who were a little older did. I remember wearing skirts most of the time with pants underneath, and I had a little scarf to cover my hair. My grandmother would wear a full *hijab*, or face covering, when she went out of the house so that all you could see was her eyes.

She didn't go out of the house very much except to visit people. My grandfather, on the other hand, owned a fruit stand, and my older uncles had a knife-sharpening business. They would travel around or set up in the souk with their big rock wheel sharpener, pedaling to make it turn and sharpen knives.

Our home was somewhat comparable to a townhouse in the U.S. We shared walls with neighbors on both sides, and all of the homes had open courtyards in the middle. All the rooms had roofs, but the middle of the house had no ceilings. I loved when it rained, because sometimes the courtyard would fill with water and we could swim in it. We had no vehicle or house phone and one black and white TV, but we were never allowed to watch it unless my grandparents turned it on.

Our one bathroom housed a Turkish toilet, which is a toilet you don't sit on, you squat over it. We didn't have toilet paper, but we did have a bucket next to it with a faucet over it to wash our hands. The other bathroom had a tub, but the water heater never worked, so we bathed once a week in the public bathhouses, or the *hammam*. They were separated into men's and women's sides, and you had to pay to get in. We all went together and brought our towels, shampoo, soap and clean clothes. Once inside, everyone would undress, get a bucket and get water out of the big tubs inside, sit down on the floor and wash themselves. There were three sections to the bathhouses—the first had cooler water, the second was warmer and the third was hot like a sauna.

Hygiene was almost nonexistent—our bath once a week was about it. None of us ever saw a dentist, and the only times I remember going to a regular doctor was to get vaccines. My grandmother had a more natural approach to medicine—she used lemon halves tied to your head with a bandanna for a headache, a teaspoon of warm olive oil or mint tea with honey for a sore throat and garlic oil for an ear infection. She was known in the community as a natural healer, and people would come to her with their ailments for her remedies.

There were a few rare moments when I was sick or very tired where my grandmother would actually be kind to me. One time, I had a reaction to a vaccine I got at the hospital, and she was concerned about me. There are also a few nights where I can remember sitting in the middle of the open courtyard all together as a family to try to get some air in the oppressive heat. She would let me lay my head in her lap, and she rubbed it until I fell asleep.

I also remember a few occasions where she actually gave me a compliment. I wasn't afraid of most normal things kids were afraid of, given my upbringing; I was tougher, raised in the streets. One time, I found a snake in the house and grabbed it by the head, and another time I did the same thing with a mouse. Both times I brought them to her, and I remember her saying, "This girl is fearless!"

She also complimented me on the way I danced. I loved music, I think because it was how I could feel free for just a moment and forget about my problems. She would say to people, "No one dances like Karima, she is the best dancer."

I was also a strong little girl; all of us kids had chores to do around the house, and one of mine was carrying the big heavy floor rugs to the spot where we would wash them, since we hand washed everything. I can also remember mopping the tile floor, folding clothes and running errands for my grandmother. Another one of my chores was to take the bread she made to the local public *ferrane*, or oven, to be baked for our meals and to pick it up when it was done.

We didn't have an oven in the house, so my grandmother cooked on something similar to the portable gas burner you can get for camping. The food was served on a big round plate for everyone to share. Men had to eat separately from women and children, but we all ate with our hands. My grandmother wouldn't allow us to have unsupervised snacks in between meals, so eating whenever we could was a no-brainer.

Couscous, which is tiny grains of pasta, was one of the main foods we ate, along with lamb or beef, sometimes chicken, veggies and different kinds of sauces. We also ate a lot of *tagines*, or stews. Dates were a common breakfast food, and one of the best foods I remember were Moroccan pancakes, or *baghrir*, with honey—they are delicious. Everyone drank a lot of black tea with mint and sugar, and coffee was a popular beverage too. We weren't allowed to have alcohol or pork, as those were forbidden under Islam. Lunch was the biggest meal of the day, and dinner was normally very light, either leftovers or just soup.

Another Moroccan snack food I loved were these little baguette sandwiches with tomato and tuna. They were another one of those foods my aunt and I would buy with a little of our begging money, and we would scarf them down before we went back home.

Once my mom and stepdad moved to France, they only made the three-day drive down to Marrakech once a year every summer for a month. Those visits were like Christmas for me.

Mom brought gifts for all of us—clothes, shoes, perfume, candy—these were the only times any of us got gifts of any kind or any new clothes. Even though my grandmother always made her open her suitcase full of gifts in front of her so she could supervise and control the gift-giving, it was still the most exciting time of the year.

Sometimes, Mom would even take us on little trips when they were in town. Marrakech is close to the Atlas Mountains, which is such a beautiful area, so she and my stepdad would take all of us in their SUV. We piled ten or twelve of us into seven seats and had the time of our lives getting away from the house and visiting the countryside with them.

When my mom was there, I wasn't beaten, woken up at 4 a.m., made to do any chores or sent out on any types of "missions." Her visits were literal heaven to me. I remember just holding on to her, breathing in her scent, wishing there was some way she could stay.

I would take any opportunity to sit by her and soak her presence in. She had no idea what my life was like as soon as she walked out the door. Every time she left, I was heartbroken. All my heart wanted was to be with her. I would cry for days before she left as I dreaded the loss of her unknowing protection.

As I reflect on that chapter of my life now, my heart goes out to all the little girls like me who are trapped in the lifestyle I was trapped in. Maybe not all are abused like I was, but living each day having to beg for your food is bad enough by itself. My heart aches for all the young boys, many homeless, wandering the streets with no protection or direction. I remember many of them walking around with their hands cupped around something close to their face, which later I found out is how they get the cheapest high—from sniffing glue. One day, I want to go back and help these children, these kids who are lost, unprotected, and don't know how to escape on their own.

Chapter 4

A Faraway God

This is love: not that we loved God, but that he loved us and sent his Son as an atoning sacrifice for our sins.
—1 John 4:10

A big part of my upbringing in Morocco was the Muslim religion—it was my identity, affecting every part of our culture and home life. Feeling like I didn't belong anywhere for so long made me cling to it even more—it was the best way I had to define who I was.

I didn't have to do a whole lot with it since I was so young when I lived in Morocco, but I watched my family do the thirty-day fast for *Ramadan* and pray to Allah five times every day. Those things are only required of children once they are around twelve years old, and since I didn't hit puberty until after I left, I never had to do any of it.

It was never explained to me why we did things the way we did them; there was no communication about any of it. This was just who we were and what we did. Everything was a ritual to us, at least that's what I thought every time I heard the *"Allah Akbar"* prayers chanted five times a day. My aunts and uncles and I knew that if we asked questions, we would get yelled at or beaten by my grandmother, so we did our best to keep quiet and do what we knew to do.

Because very few were educated, most religious traditions were verbally passed down. No one knew the truth of why we did what we did, because what they did had been told to them by their parents and by their parents before them. There was no comparing what was told to you as truth to a sermon, or even the actual Quran, since most people couldn't read. That is probably one of the reasons I never prayed for Allah to help me; I wasn't taught to pray like that.

Every religious behavior was an outward show. I would watch my grandmother pray and then turn around and cuss somebody out, so I had no reason to believe that Allah was a good god or cared about any of us. I never thought of him as a father, or anyone I could go to for comfort or help. The thought never crossed my mind to think of him in that way. I remember thinking that if my grandmother worshiped Allah and could treat me so horribly, why would I want to worship a god who could allow her to do that?

Honestly, I was almost as scared of him as I was of my grandmother. I thought he was powerful, but I doubted he had any idea who I was. My grandmother was alive and right in front of me, and Allah was off somewhere in the sky.

There is no love or any type of intimate relationship between Muslims and Allah, at least from my experience with the religion. Allah was up there, I was down here. I was told if I didn't do and say and pray all the things I was told, I would go to hell. I prayed out of fearful respect for him; I had no love for him or relationship with him.

Respect is a huge part of the Muslim religion, and we were expected to show it to our elders. My aunts and uncles and I had to kiss my grandparents on their foreheads and hands, and I was expected to do the same thing for my uncles. I could kiss other women on the cheeks or hug them, but I couldn't hug any boys or men outside of the family.

I never saw any outward expressions of love or affection among my family or was ever told "I love you" in all my growing up years. I never saw any married family members kiss while in Morocco—even in the Egyptian movies we sometimes watched, there was absolutely no kissing, PDA, or nudity.

Islam is also the reason why we all dressed the way we did and ate separately at meals. All the women were separated from the men for most things, and women didn't go out as much as men. It wasn't common to see women out in the cafes, and if a woman was with a man, they had better be married or they could both end up in jail.

Parental respect also played out in traditional marriages; back then, almost all marriages were still arranged by the parents. My grandmother arranged marriages for almost every one of her kids, including my uncles. She turned down many suitors for my aunts, which I suspect was because she didn't want to lose them from her household. My aunt who is closest in age to me is still unmarried to this day, because my grandmother would not allow it.

In my estimation, my aunts were trapped by the fear of my grandmother, coupled with the mandate for religious respect, and in many ways they still are to this day. We were all trapped to some degree by her expectations and our own consequential low self-esteem.

We had five major Muslim holidays that we celebrated: *El Reid Sahir*, which came right after the month of fasting for

Ramadan; *Eid al-Fitr*, Muslim New Year; *Mawlid al-Nabi*, celebrating the birth of the prophet Muhammed; and *El Reid El kbir*, which was our biggest holiday and the one I liked the least. My grandparents would buy a sheep, which we would keep in the house with us for a few weeks to fatten him up. Then, the butcher would be called to kill it for a sacrifice, which he would do right in the center of our home. There was blood everywhere, and after the sacrifice was over we would have the meat to eat for several weeks. The whole holiday was based on the Bible story in Genesis when God tells Abraham to sacrifice Isaac but provides a ram instead as the sacrifice.

My favorite part about holidays was all the different desserts we enjoyed. Of course, my grandmother hid all of them under her bed and we were never allowed to have any unless we had guests over to the house. Naturally, my youngest aunt and I worked out a system to steal from her. My grandmother had chickens in an upstairs room of the house, so when she fed them one of us acted as sentry while the other snatched the sweets.

All of us lied to her and hid things from her. We made it into a game sometimes, which was fun until we got caught. Even when we were all adults, I remember visiting her later in life and one of my uncles sneaking in some food. We were and still are to this day bonded by our shared trauma.

On top of religion, Moroccans are also very superstitious. I remember certain things that sound silly now, but they were very serious to people there, like how we were not ever supposed to open an umbrella in our house. Owning a black cat was unthinkable, and even if you saw one, we were taught that it was an omen, or sign, that someone close to you was going to die.

My grandmother had this little charcoal barbeque pit in her room, and she would take these clear rocks and burn them. Whatever shape they made, she would somehow translate into knowing all the people who wanted to hurt you or were jealous of you. She also used it once in a while to cleanse us of the "evil eye"—she took white alum stone, turned it around our head seven times, said a prayer and then put it in the pit to burn. She also burned a lot of incense, and despite my fear of her, I loved her smell—she always smelled good from all the incense and oils she burned.

My aunt and I even had a little superstition for when we thought we had a beating waiting for us at home. Each of us would pick up a pebble from the road, put it under our tongues and say our little rock prayer: "Quiet rock, don't let my mother tell me a word." Basically, we thought it might make my grandmother leave us alone—sometimes it worked, sometimes it didn't. (This shows how little I felt I could count on Allah…I was out there praying for rocks to save me. I had zero faith in his ability or desire to help me.)

Islam was also reinforced at school—it was the primary thing we learned. I can still recite many of the prayers I learned from the Quran, because even at a young age we were expected to memorize many parts of it. In our equivalent of pre-K, all the children would sit on the floor with boards and chalk, writing *surah*, or chapters of the Quran, in order to memorize them. I remember rocking back and forth on the floor with all the other kids, chanting the prayers we were learning together.

We didn't have any gym, PE, recreational time or a library at school. It was all classes and learning and Quran memorization, and after class was over all the kids went straight home. I was a pretty good kid at school and laid low, and since we didn't have any free time, I didn't interact much with any of the other kids my age.

I was more terrified of my grandmother receiving a bad report about me than I was of any consequences from the school for bad behavior. My fear of her truly overflowed into every area of life. I remember her telling me, "Your dad's family doesn't want you. They always told your mom to throw you in the ocean. That's the kind of family you have. Your dad is going to come and steal you away from school one day." Of course, that only made things worse. Unfortunately, at that time there was no equivalent of a school guidance counselor to help me. But truth be told, I would have been too afraid to talk to one anyway.

I was the only one of the kids in the house to even go to school; I think my grandmother knew that if she didn't send me and my mom found out, my mom would stop sending money.

Visiting temples, or *zawiyas*, as well as *mosques*, was also a part of my upbringing. There was no regularity to it, but I remember going to different ones every once in a while. Each one was associated with a certain *shaykh* (religious leader) or *wali* (local Muslim saint), who was buried there along with his family. People would go in there and walk around, and if you prayed, the prayers would be recited from the Quran. The temple in Marrakech called *Sidi Abdelaziz* is one that I remember visiting. It was about a mile away from my grandmother's house, and the only detail I remember is seeing many beggars outside.

One temple I remember was out in the country where one of my older uncles lived. His house was a clay and stone building, with sheets covering the windows and doorways. There was no running water or electricity there at the time; they used candles or lanterns. There was an area outside the building for a bathroom, if you could even call it that. It was just a hole in the ground, and once it was full, the contents would be burned to "empty" it. Needless to say, the whole area outside smelled horrible.

Even worse, the temple there left a mark on my young mind. It's called the *Bouya Omar Mausoleum*, and I remember seeing people chained up outside, some foaming at the mouth and acting crazy. It wasn't until much later that I learned how some temples were used like insane asylums, where people would send mentally disabled family members for "treatment" that was actually an abusive nightmare. These types of places don't exist any more, but with the lack of psychiatric health care in that time, many atrocities were committed against innocent people. The memory of that temple is seared into my brain—it was such a frightening, unsettling experience.

At my grandparents' house in Marrakesh, celebrating my 4th birthday

Age 10, Mom took me to get my picture taken in a studio, since we did not have any cameras back then

Chapter 5

Free at Last

God sets the lonely in families, he leads out the prisoners with singing... —Psalm 68:6

Age 12, on the ferry, traveling to France for the first time

On my mom's visit in the summer of 1986, when I was twelve, the family was celebrating my cousin's circumcision. For Moroccan culture, a circumcision is a big celebration. Most of my family members and our family friends were there, people were cooking all day and someone even hired a group to come sing and play music. I was so excited—it was going to be such a good day, and most importantly, my mom was home.

I remember dancing around the house that day, feeling so free, almost forgetting the prison I was living in. Suddenly, my grandmother came out of nowhere and grabbed me.

I'm not sure what happened exactly, but my grandmother got very angry at me, so much so that she forgot who was there or what was going on. She grabbed onto the collar of my special party dress my mom had bought me and began screaming at me and wouldn't let go.

This caught my mom and stepdad's attention right away. Just as she was about to hit me, my stepdad came and grabbed her arm and said, "No! You can't hit her." I remember my mom yelling, "Let go of her!" but my grandmother refused to let go of my dress.

They argued loudly, and finally, my mom snatched me away, tearing my dress. My stepdad was shocked that my grandmother would treat me that way. My mom had never seen my grandmother be mean to me in any way until that day. I saw her fierce motherly instincts kick in, for which I will be eternally grateful. They argued for a while, and I remember my mom yelling those life-altering words at my grandmother:

"I'm taking my daughter with me!"

My grandmother promptly kicked the three of us out of the house.

That day went from feeling like a celebration to feeling like a funeral in the span of minutes. I was in disbelief at what was happening, and I think everyone else was too. Many of our family members were crying and upset about what was happening, and one of my aunts later told me how they all felt so sick as we left and walked out the door.

It was such a big deal to them that this was happening, not as much that I was leaving but more that my mom was leaving, and leaving so angry at my grandmother. As the oldest daughter, she was like a mother to her siblings, the mother my grandmother never was. Her visits were the only bright spot in a very dark life for them, just as they were for me. She cared about them, loved them, and brought them gifts. They were being abandoned—left alone, with no hope and nothing to look forward to.

I don't think I realized what it all meant until my mom, my stepdad and I walked out the door, down the street, and away from that house of terror and abuse. I was truly freed from prison that day.

They took me back to Mohammedia to get permission from my biological dad to let me travel to France, which is when we found out that he had passed away two years earlier from heart problems. We were stunned, as no one had told us until then. If he had been alive, I don't think he would have let me leave the country—not because he cared, but because of his abusiveness and anger towards my mom. I didn't understand the impact of his death on me until I was much older; all I knew was that now we could get my paperwork done so that I could get my passport and finally leave the country with my family.

Once we had my passport in hand and our bags packed, my mom, stepdad, and I left for France. Riding in their Nissan

Patrol, the trip took three whole days. We drove all the way to the northern shore of Morocco and took a ferry from Tanger, Morocco to Malaga, Spain before driving the rest of the way to southern France.

I remember that part of the journey vividly. The balmy Mediterranean breeze kissed my cheeks as I breathed in the salty air and held onto the railing for dear life. I had never been on a boat before, so I was a little nervous!

My emotions and thoughts were everywhere; a part of me was sad and scared to leave the only home, country, language, and family I knew. On the other hand, a dream of mine was finally coming true—one I never dared to hope would happen. I was leaving Morocco *with my mom*. I couldn't stop smiling every time that thought crossed my mind. Finally, I was with her, and no one could take me away. In the pictures I have of me on the boat, I look nervous, but I'm smiling, like the excitement and awe were just enough to overshadow any fears I had at the moment.

Eventually, we arrived at the tiny village of Sergines, a ninety minute drive from Paris in the countryside of France. As we drove in, I was awestruck. The village, with a population of only 1300, was surrounded by open fields, ablaze with vibrant *tournesols*, or sunflowers. Wheat fields rippled in the breeze under the bright blue sky—I thought I was in paradise. I had never seen anything like this in Morocco, living in a bustling city where the intense heat made most of the vegetation dry and brown.

We pulled up at a campground next to a small, cozy-looking camper. Inside was a bedroom, living room, dining room, one bathroom, a kitchen, and another smaller bedroom—more like a closet with bunk beds. They were tiny, only about two to three feet wide. But I wasn't about to complain. As I laid down in one of them, a wave of peace flowed over me and my new reality truly sank in. I wasn't going to be kicked awake anymore. There wasn't going to be any more screaming, any more 4 a.m. wake-up calls. I could wake up and see my mom *every day*. I had my own area, all to myself, and I felt safe and protected. I couldn't have been more grateful.

My parents lived in the trailer since my dad traveled constantly for his job. It made it easier to have a portable home so they could be flexible with his work and travel more comfortably together. However, after I moved in with them, my mom gave up traveling with him to stay and take care of me.

We arrived in the middle of the summer, so I had plenty of time to get settled in before school started in the fall. Soon after we moved, my parents bought me my first toy ever—a beautiful Barbie doll that I still have to this day. I had never owned or played with any toys before, only in my imagination. I was over-the-moon happy. My Barbie had a long, flowing gown that glowed at night; I thought it was the coolest thing ever, and it was so very special to me.

The negative consequences of my move really didn't start to hit me until that September when I started school. I started there in 6th grade, which was a year behind where I was in Morocco. It was pretty intimidating, not only going to a brand new school with new kids, but also having a brand new language and culture to learn.

After I took a bus for the first time, I got to school and started realizing how hard it was going to be. Back in Morocco, I prided myself on how good I was at school. There, I was always at the top of my class. I loved learning, but in France, the teachers taught unaware that I didn't speak or understand French. There were no guidance counselors at the time, and I don't remember the teachers helping me in any way. To make matters worse, my mom couldn't even help me with homework since she had never been to school and couldn't read or write. My stepdad was gone traveling for work almost all the time, so I was left to struggle alone.

Not only was I learning two completely new languages (French and English), but I was also having to write completely differently. In Arabic, I wrote right to left, in characters that look nothing like our English or French alphabet. Now, I was having to write left to right, which was really hard to wrap my mind around.

I also didn't know how to ask for help. Back in Morocco, the extent of my communication with adults in my household was being yelled at and avoiding confrontation, which in turn forced me to do everything on my own. I did all my homework by myself and never asked for help, and yet I always finished first or second in my class. Since that was the way I had always done things, I subconsciously continued to adapt that same method in France. Seeking help was as foreign to me as the new language and culture I found myself in.

We didn't have any extracurricular activities or clubs, but we did have a chorus class. Even though I couldn't understand what we were singing, my love for music made that class a bright spot in my days, and we even got to do an end-of-year concert for it.

On top of my struggle to understand what was happening at school, I also looked different from every other kid. I was either picked on or ignored, so at school I was mostly quiet and lonely. I had long, black hair all the way down my back, which got pulled regularly, especially by the boys on the bus. A lot of kids called me "barracuda" since my last name was Baraka.

My self-esteem being abysmal after growing up with my grandmother, I was hard on myself. I thought I was stupid. I told myself I didn't measure up. I yearned to be white, to have light hair, to look like the other girls, to be able to understand them and relate to them. I have always been petite—when I was fourteen, I looked like I was ten. In my mind, I looked like a little boy, and I constantly compared myself to the other kids, wishing so hard that I could be more like them, wishing for all the things I didn't have.

I met one kind soul at school, Aude, who became my best friend that year. She was about a year older than me, but so kind and accepting of me and helped me learn the language, even though I could barely communicate with her. She called me *perruque*, or "wig," because I had such long hair, and I called her *squelette*, or "skeleton," because she was so skinny. Her family lived in my village, so we saw each other a lot and became close. I vividly remember one time I was over at her house and had macaroni pasta with ketchup for dinner—it was a strange meal to me at the time, as I was still adjusting to French food.

There were so many new types of food I had never tried, like *langue de vache* (cow tongue), *cerveau de vache* (cow brain), *steak de cheval* (horse steak) and *boudin noir* (blood sausage). I was not a big fan of the meats, but I did love a lot of the desserts and pastries, like *flan, mille-feuille* and *tarte au fruit.* One of my favorite French bakery items is the classic *baguette.* However, Moroccan food was definitely still my comfort food, even though I enjoyed trying some new things.

The culture was so different from Morocco, too—my parents didn't follow any religion with any type of regularity. We all ate together, instead of the women being separated from the men, and everyone had their own plate instead of sharing from a big communal bowl. Men and women talked to each other a lot more in France, and modesty was not as strict as it was in Morocco either. Nudity was common on TV, and women in France didn't wear head-to-toe coverings outside.

With all the overwhelming changes happening in my life, the highlight of my days was coming back home to my mom, or *Maman,* as I called her once I moved. She always had a snack waiting for me, normally cookies and apple juice. I had such peace and comfort from knowing she would always be there when I got home and that she would never leave me again.

She would cook Moroccan food for me still, and we would speak Arabic together. And I still danced to Moroccan music. All of that added to my feeling of being so safe at home with her, in a culture I recognized and loved.

She was such an amazing mom to me and still is; but I especially remember being so thankful for her when I initially moved to France. I felt like she and my stepdad had saved me from my horrible life in Morocco. She took such good care of me. If anything, she was over-protective, since she had been without me for so long that she was a little afraid of losing me, the same way I felt like this life with her was just too good to be true. I put all the stealing and lying behind me, and focused on being as good a daughter to her and my stepdad as I could be.

That winter, I visited my stepdad's family for the holidays for the first time. They lived in Verdun, about a four hour drive north of our home. It was such a beautiful, scenic drive that

I didn't mind how long it was. They were all so sweet, gentle and welcoming—especially my new grandmother, or *mamie* as I called her. I was touched by her kindness to me, since it was so different from what I experienced with the only other grandmother I had known.

I felt as though I gained a whole new family of aunts, uncles, cousins and a grandmother, and I loved spending holidays with them. We would have big meals together and play games as a whole group. They were all incredibly generous to me, giving me lots of Christmas gifts or money each year. At Easter, my grandmother would hide chocolate eggs all over her yards for us to find, which my cousins and I loved.

I spent the most time with one of my dad's brother's family, since he had two boys and a girl my age. We listened to music and played together, and they were all so kind and understanding with me even though I couldn't really speak French well yet. One of my favorite memories of spending time with their family is how their mom would make us brioche and Nutella for breakfast.

Another one of my favorite memories from that first year in Sergines also happened in wintertime. One cold winter day, I walked outside, and little white flakes were falling from the sky! Experiencing snow for the first time was magical. It covered our little village in a white blanket and made everything look so beautiful. I wasn't really sure how to play in it, but my stepdad came outside with me and taught me how to make snowballs. We had a snowball fight, and I laughed and screamed with abandon. My mom bought me a little blue snowsuit and pink gloves, which she still has in her house today.

Chapter 6

Late Bloomer

For I know the plans I have for you," declares the LORD, "plans to prosper you and not to harm you, plans to give you hope and a future. —Jeremiah 29:11

After that first school year was over, my mom and stepdad decided to buy an actual home, since my mom was now staying with me while my stepdad traveled. The house they found was in an even smaller village called St. Martin, about 14 kilometers away from our first home and 90 minutes south of Paris. In the new home, I had my own room, which I remember being so excited about. It was a large house with plenty of rooms and it sat on a one-acre lot with a fenced yard.

My mom started gardening there, and since I was gone at school all day and my stepdad was traveling for work so often, it filled a lot of her spare time. She grew all kinds of vegetables, and we even had several fruit trees. What developed over time was a little farm, since she also bought rabbits, chickens, and turkeys. I loved living there, going through the daily rhythms of life with my mom.

Soon after our move, we had a new addition to our family—my first sister, and not long after, my second little sister in 1989. My mom had been trying to get pregnant for a long time, back when I was still in Morocco. She had two miscarriages before I moved to France, which she thinks could have been related to how much stress and anxiety she felt because I was not living with her.

There were downsides to our move, of course. I had to move to a new school, so I didn't see my friend, Aude, very much anymore. We hung out every once in a while on the weekends, staying up until two in the morning talking. We also talked on the phone sometimes since our parents both had house phones, but it wasn't enough and I wished so much that she could come to my new school with me.

Also, since the village was so small, there were hardly any people out walking around, and even fewer kids to play with. When we walked down the street, it felt like a Western movie—all the window shutters were closed, and it felt too quiet, almost abandoned. Many of the people who owned houses there lived in Paris and only visited on the weekends. I met one such family with two little girls, Celine and Stephanie, who I played with occasionally.

Since my mom didn't have her driver's license, we also couldn't go to the market as easily as I could in Morocco. There was a bus that would come to our village every Monday that would take people to the nearest bigger town with a market, and then pick them up and take them back home later in the day, but that was it. Other than that, we were stuck right where we were.

School continued to be rough—I had failed that first year in Sergines and had to repeat the 6th grade at my new school. Even though I could speak French pretty well by then, doing school work at that grade level was a constant struggle. By the time I got a better grip on the language and could understand more, I was so far behind.

With all the changes in my life that year and the challenges I continued to face adapting to a new culture, country, language and home, I was behind the curve growing up, so I was referred to as a *garcon manquer*, or tomboy, during those early years in France. I wore mostly pants and shirts, which made me look more like a boy. I didn't really start wearing dresses or putting makeup on until I was around 15 years old. I think that was partially due to how I was raised in Morocco—I didn't think about what I wore or how I looked, since I didn't have a choice. I was kept younger than my age under the control of my grandmother, and having to focus on stealing and begging also robbed me of a childhood. When you go from someone telling you when and how to eat, sleep, and react to being able to make all those choices on your own, it's confusing.

I tried to hang on to childhood while also experiencing these changes—for example, I didn't stop playing with my Barbie until I was around fourteen. There were so many new things for me to learn about life and my body on top of all the changes from moving to a new country that it took me a little longer to grow up, look my age and realize the new freedoms I had.

Those first three years in France were a time of internal transitioning for me. I realize now how much our culture values self-expression, and parents are encouraged to help their kids become a unique person, to express themselves and find their gifts and talents. Because my childhood was totally the opposite, I was behind on all of those things, so my early teenage years were focused on figuring out who I was and who I could become.

The positive aspect of this change was that my mom knew how to love me, despite also being raised by the same unloving parent I had for the first twelve years of my life. She didn't use life's challenges as an excuse to be horrible to people the way my grandmother did. She and my stepdad created a loving, supportive environment for me to grow up in, and I'm so thankful for the love my parents showed me and continue to show me now.

My days in St. Martin became pretty routine—my mom would wake me up with music and make me breakfast, and I would head to the bus station about a half mile down the road and ride the bus to school, which was in a bigger town 12 kilometers away. We had classes and then lunch in the cafeteria, and a 30 minute "recess" in the big courtyard at the school in the middle of the day, where I would play ping pong in my free time. It was better than my day-to-day life in Morocco, but I still felt lonely and out of place.

I had thought that moving to a new country, finally living with my mom, and getting out of Morocco and my grandmother's house would make me feel satisfied. How could I have anticipated all the other variables that moving to a new country would introduce into my life, especially as a naive little girl. Don't get me wrong, I was deeply thankful for all the positives that came with my new life, especially being with my mom—but I didn't understand why I still felt like I didn't belong. I looked, sounded, and felt different from all the kids my age. I couldn't succeed in school and was made fun of by the other kids I so desperately wanted to be like. In many ways, I was still an outsider.

Religion wasn't filling that void for me either. After my mom left Morocco, the only Islamic ritual she still practiced was Ramadan. She didn't pray or do any of the incense burning my grandmother did. My stepdad didn't practice any religion that I saw—later in life, I found out he was raised Catholic. Almost every village in France has a beautiful cathedral, but I don't remember my stepdad ever going to mass. In my experience, most French people subscribed to but didn't practice Catholicism.

We did celebrate Christmas and Easter, and my parents even had a little nativity scene they would set up under our Christmas tree. However, just as with Islam, I had no idea why we did any of the religious things we did. All I knew was that I got presents at Christmas and chocolate at Easter.

When I was around fourteen, I started thinking about Allah more, and wondering if I should be doing anything religious. I still had a little fear of him, so I was worried I was missing something important I was supposed to do. I remember one time specifically when I asked my mom about it, she told me, "Karima, all you have to do is be a good person—that's all that matters." I had a lot of trust in my mom and what she told me, and I wondered if in escaping Morocco, I had escaped Allah's reach too. I put all the stealing and lying behind me, and tried my very best to do exactly what my mom said, but it still didn't fill the void inside me.

That following summer, the summer of 1988, we made our first trip back to Morocco since my move to France. Because of the tension from our last visit, my mom decided to skip the first summer trip after we moved. I don't remember much, but I am told that my grandmother greeted us with open arms. She and my mom never discussed what happened that day we left in 1986. It was a great family vacation, and we went back as usual every summer after that.

While we were there, I remember eating meals together, shopping in the souk and playing music and dancing with everyone. We wore long dresses to please my grandmother and retreated to our rooms at prayer times to make her think we were still praying to Allah. It was strange being there not having to get up early to steal or beg. I felt so protected by my mom; I continued feeling afraid of my grandmother, who still screamed and yelled at people, but at least it didn't feel like she could hurt me. I wasn't excited to be back, and it was hard to relax and have a good time, but I loved seeing my aunts and uncles again.

My heart definitely went out to them—I felt a tinge of guilt sharing things about my new life in France with them. They were all very happy for me though, even though they had been stranded from my mom, the one family member who actually cared about any of them. She still sent money to help them out and some small gifts, but not as much as when I was living there.

My one aunt told me that a couple weeks after I had left, she was hit while stealing in the market one morning. She decided that she had enough, and went home and told my grandmother that the market added police officers, and they were taking people who stole things to jail. It was all made up, but my grandmother believed her and never again sent my aunts out to the 5 a.m. market. I laughed and asked why she couldn't have thought of that when I still lived there with them.

Back in France that fall, school actually got a little better for me, in a backwards kind of way. I had failed that past second year of school as well, which was my second failed year of the same grade. By then, I was too old to stay in that grade, so in the fall of 1988, when I was fourteen, I was moved to an intermediate "hands-on" class. It was the only option for me since I had failed out of sixth grade, but I loved those classes.

Failing was a blessing in disguise for me. There, in addition to History, Math, French, English, etc., I learned how to cook, build things and do projects. I even made an outdoor light fixture for my parents' home, which is still there today. Finally, I felt like I could understand and accomplish some of what I was supposed to do.

My favorite class was always Physical Education, since I was actually good at it. I got to show off my strength, which boosted my self-esteem. I had the fastest time of my whole class for climbing the big rope in the gym, and I was also great at gymnastics. All those years doing hard chores in Morocco paid off.

We didn't have any sports teams—the whole class did the same PE, from gymnastics and swimming to tennis and rugby. France is actually where I learned how to swim, since there were no pools where I was in Morocco. There was a public pool close to the school, so the teacher would walk our class over to swim. There were also no clubs, dances or even a picture day or yearbook. It was better than in Morocco, where we had no type of extracurricular activities, but I still tell my kids now how lucky they are to grow up in the modern American education system, with all the different things it has to offer compared to other countries back then.

I was in the "hands on" classes for two years. The second year of these classes was when I started an apprenticeship for hair styling. I had always loved doing my hair, so as one of my classes I helped out at a salon doing odd jobs, like sweeping up and answering phones. Even though I wasn't paid for my work, I loved being there and tried to learn as much as I could about doing hair.

I didn't get my driver's license until I turned 18, so my stepdad bought me a moped to get between my classes at the high school and my apprenticeship. My mom couldn't drive either, so when my stepdad traveled, I would sometimes help her pick up groceries for the family.

Another perk of having the moped was that I started riding it to the gym and working out. I didn't really do much cardio; I mainly lifted weights, inspired by Arnold Schwarzenegger. I had always been very strong, so working out became a fun outlet for me to do something I loved and was good at.

It was a little scary riding my moped at night back to my mom's after my later shifts at the salon. I was afraid something would come out of the woods and get me. One late afternoon when I was making the trip home, I was coming up a gravely hill by the entrance to some woods and wiped out. My elbows and knees were full of gravel, scraped and bleeding. My moped wouldn't start back up, and as it got darker I became terrified. I was only still 16 at the time and had no way of getting help, since no one had cell phones at the time. Thankfully, a kind couple eventually drove by and took me and my bike home.

That wasn't my worst accident, though. Every once in a while, St. Martin would have these little gatherings, or *Kermesse*, where everyone who lived in the village would come, and there would be food and music—a festival of sorts—for a charitable purpose. Since my village was so small and I didn't socialize with anyone outside school, my mom always wanted me to go.

I remember one Saturday in particular when my mom asked me if I wanted to go. As a young teen, I already had my own idea of what I wanted to do, which was to go to the public pool in the city near us. My mom insisted that I go to the festival. Infuriated, I stormed out of the house.

I don't know what came over me. I saw my friend's bicycle outside her house at the top of our cul-de-sac, so I hopped on and started riding down the hill. It wasn't until I was whizzing by my house at full speed that I realized the bike had no brakes. I panicked, closed my eyes and yelled "I don't have any brakes!" I noticed two of our neighbors were standing outside their homes out of the corner of my eye, as I headed straight for the wheelbarrow leaned against one of the houses. The bike crashed into the wheelbarrow, catapulting me into the concrete wall of the house.

I woke up in the car on the way to the hospital in so much pain. I could feel the blood trickling down my face. It was warm and sticky, and had a metallic taste in my mouth. My neighbors said later that I hit the wheelbarrow so hard that I lost consciousness immediately. One of them picked me up and carried me home, unconscious and blood everywhere. My mom was terrified, but thankfully my stepdad was home to take me to the hospital. I remember waking up in the car and feeling my teeth, having an out-of-body experience as I noticed some of them were broken and chipped. I thought I was dreaming as I passed in and out of consciousness.

I ended up having surgery and spending two weeks in the hospital for recovery. I had a fake tooth, and they were only able to do a little to fix my nose, since I was still growing; it was tender and misshapen for years. I could barely wear sunglasses to cover my bruised eyes because of the pressure—another added challenge to looking different at school. If I had any self-esteem left at that point, my accident destroyed the rest. I was a petite 5'3", Arabic, with thick, curly black hair and a big nose. All the most beautiful French girls were more developed, tall and blonde with white skin and blue eyes. I continued wishing every minute of every day that I could be more like them.

When I was fifteen, Whitney Houston helped inspire me to change something about my appearance that I had been wanting to do for so long—cut my hair. I had finally convinced my mom to let me cut off my long, thick black hair; she loved it long and never wanted me to cut it. But all the girls in school had short hair, so I cut it all off into a bob just like Whitney, who I thought was so beautiful.

I remember buying magazines in France that didn't help with any of the discontent I was struggling with. I looked at all the beautiful women on the pages and made myself sick to my stomach wishing I looked like them. (I realize now they were all airbrushed, but for a young girl like me who had little to no self-confidence, I held these women up as the standard to achieve.)

Of course, watching TV also added to my unrealistic perception of what women were supposed to look like. My mom loves American soap operas, so I grew up watching those, along with my dad's American westerns. I also started listening to American music from Whitney Houston, Celine Dion and others, but my favorite was Michael Jackson. I could never understand what the singers were saying, but I mimicked their voices as best as I could! Sometimes, I closed myself in my room with only my boom box and cassette player to keep me company, listening to music and singing for hours.

Music was the best way I knew to cope with all the feelings I had inside about not belonging. My dream of going to America one day only grew stronger after moving to France, especially after watching all the American TV shows with my parents showing all the beautiful, rich people there. I thought America was this beautiful, strong, amazing country—the most powerful country in the world! I loved the way their language sounded and was enchanted by their culture.

Deep down inside, my heart still yearned to be loved one day the way I saw the foreign men in the souk loving their wives. Inside, I still felt like that wide-eyed, little, forgotten Moroccan girl—alone, waiting to finally belong somewhere.

Chapter 7

American Dreaming

For God so loved the world that he gave his only begotten Son, that whosoever believeth in him should not perish, but have everlasting life. —John 3:16

After two years of the "hands-on" classes, it was time for me to move on from high school. I had so many career dreams, but because I didn't pass high school, my options were limited. In 1990 when I was 16 years old, I enrolled in a technical college about an hour away from my parents' home, working towards a Master Cosmetologist degree. I thought it would be a good fit for me, especially after having done my apprenticeship that last year of high school.

It was a public college, but since it was an hour away from our house my parents paid for me to live on campus. The way the classes worked, I was there for two weeks, then home working in the salon for two weeks, so my stepdad or one of my parents' neighbors drove me back and forth every other weekend. Since that was the way the classes worked, the other students were from all over France.

When I was there, I shared a dorm room with two other girls, but we barely talked. I was so insecure about my social status, so I kept to myself and went about my business. I did make one good friend there—her name was Veronique, and her family was from South Africa. She was in the same classes as me, so we would help each other out with school work, and even visited each other's homes a few times.

I had several core classes, like Math, Science, Grammar, Social Studies, and I even started learning English. In addition to those, I also had my hair classes, where I learned how to cut, color and perm hair. I chose the degree path that would allow me to style both men's and women's hair. At that time in France, I was told I had to do two years of school to be certified for women's hair, and one more to be certified to do men's hair. After the first two years, I was given the option to test out of that last year. I was so proud of myself when I passed and ended up graduating with my diploma in two years instead of three.

In France, there are no graduation ceremonies for any type of colleges, so when I finished I started right away working full-time at the salon where I had already been working. I turned 18 right after I graduated, so my parents threw me a big birthday party and invited all my friends. They gave me a big stereo, since they knew how much I loved music.

After graduating and turning eighteen, I couldn't wait to get out into the world, make a name for myself and live independently. My boss at the time had a small apartment above the salon, and she allowed me to live there and pay minimal rent. I missed my family, but I enjoyed the freedom of living on my own, and I was only about 12 kilometers away from them. I visited them at least two or three days a week, to catch up with them and see my little sisters.

I would often meet my friends after work to hang out at the dance club. We would sometimes start the evening at the bowling alley and then walk across the street to the club, dancing for hours until it closed early in the morning. I loved the song "Rhythm of a Dancer"—I could dance to that song all night long. Then, we'd find a bakery that was getting ready for the day, where the smell of freshly baked pastries wafted out into the street, and buy freshly made croissants. After that, we headed home, slept a few hours, and went back to work. It was crazy sometimes, but I was a teenager enjoying her freedom.

Every year in Paris, there was this big trade show for hairstylists and makeup artists to come see the new trends and make connections with other people in the field. In October of 1992, my boss took me and all my coworkers there as a work trip. We took a train into Paris, and when we arrived at the trade show we all started walking around together, visiting the different booths and learning new ways to color and cut hair.

Walking past one booth, a man stopped me and asked, "Would you like to go to America? They would love you over there!"

I was shocked. The next minute felt like an hour, like I was dreaming. Of course I wanted to go to America! That has only been my dream for my entire life! But who was this random guy? Why did he want me?

He had continued talking, explaining that he owned five hair salons and was looking for twenty-four hairstylists to go to the U.S. for an exchange program for a year and a half. He handed me an application, and told me all I had to do was fill it out. He would call to let me know if I was accepted.

Thousands of thoughts were running through my head, and I wondered if maybe he wanted to take me and put me on the streets and prostitute me—I had no idea who this guy was. I turned to my boss, who was standing there the whole time he was talking to me, and asked her what she thought. She said "He seems legit. You have nothing to lose in filling out an application. Just do it and see what happens."

As I filled it out, I thought about how I had just graduated from cosmetology school that year, and how there must be so many more applicants with more experience than me. But I finished filling it out and gave it to him anyway, trying to forget about the whole experience as I walked away with my coworkers. I thought it must be too good to be true.

I thought about it the next couple days, and I nervously hoped for them to somehow contact me. I remembered seeing a commercial on TV where a company was talking about how they were looking for hairstylists to go to America. My hope grew, thinking maybe the opportunity was legitimate. I remember thinking how it would be the most amazing dream come true, but that it would never happen to me. I was a nobody, and I assumed they probably picked the best of the best hairstylists to go.

Two days later, I got the call: I had been chosen to go to America! I was so shocked and excited, I couldn't believe what was happening to me. I called my mom in tears right away—"Mom, I'm going to America!" She was equally as shocked as me. "No way!" she said. I explained what had happened, and she was so happy for me. She knew how obsessed I was about the U.S. and how badly I wanted to go.

I know she was worried for me, too. What mom wouldn't be, sending their eighteen year-old daughter with a group of strangers to a foreign country for over a year? But she supported my enthusiasm, which I am so grateful for. I had mixed feelings telling her, and as I thought more about going, I realized I would miss her and the rest of my family so much that it physically hurt me. Having my mom in my life was still such a gift to me, and I was so thankful to have been living with her those past few years after wanting to be with her my whole childhood.

The more I thought about it, the more it killed me to think about leaving her and the rest of my family. I had several conversations about my feelings with my mom. I remember one specifically where she told me that she couldn't be the one to keep me there in France and keep me from my dreams of going to the U.S., but I was still unsure of my decision and felt torn in two. I had to choose between my two lifelong dreams—getting to live close to my mom, and going to America.

To help me make my decision, she asked if she could take me to see a psychic. Thinking about this now, it's ironic that I never once thought about praying or asking Allah for help in this decision. Looking back, it's a clear representation of where I was in my faith. I was firmly in a stage of relying on myself to be good—I still called myself a Muslim but didn't follow any of the religious requirements. I didn't know how to make this life-changing decision by myself, so I thought seeing someone who could predict my future was a great idea.

So, my mom and I went to see this lady. I clearly remember what she said, "This is what I see in your future: I see you going to Washington, D.C., and I see you meeting someone from the government. I see you're going to do very well there and have a wonderful life and eventually get married there."

Of course, I was over the moon—this was my sign. My strongest longing to be accepted and cherished by a handsome American man was finally going to come true. My thoughts flashed back to the little beggar girls in the souk longing to be loved and truly belong, watching the foreign couples hold hands as they walked through the booths. I immediately turned to my mom, and said, "I'm going to go."

Once I accepted the position, I knew I would be leaving in a few months, so I decided to move back home to spend more time with my family and have one last Christmas with them at home. The trip was scheduled to leave France the following February, so I had four months to get my visa and paperwork all straightened out. My stepdad took me on a few trips to Paris to get those things done, as well as for me to meet the team of hairstylists I would be going with and attending the pre-trip meetings.

Our travel and lodging were all paid for; they had rented out several apartments to put us up in for the first two months, but we were expected to find our own place to live after that. There was also a reimbursement plan set up, where they would take a little money out of each paycheck to cover all the costs of the travel and apartments. It was a mutually beneficial experiment, where all the hairstylists were able to go to the U.S. and get experience, and the company was getting to market their French hairstylists to their customers.

I was excited and nervous, not knowing what to expect. I was the youngest on the trip and could not speak or understand English well, which added to my stress and insecurity. I was once again leaving the country I called home, the culture I knew and language I understood to start all over again in a brand new place.

But finally, all my dreams were coming true. I was on my way to America.

Seeing snow for the first time at the camp in Sergines

At my parents' house in Saint Martin; they had just bought me the moped. I was happy but terrified at the same time to have to ride a bike to school.

Chapter 8

Finding Myself, Losing Myself

Jesus answered, "I am the way and the truth and the life.
*No one comes to the Father except through me. —*John 14:6

1993, just after arriving in Washington DC. I had to take a photo with one of the coolest American cars.

On the ten hour flight from Paris to D.C., I kept pinching myself—I still didn't believe this was really happening to me. I was in shock until I stepped off that plane and my feet were on the ground in America. My fear and excitement escalated as we deboarded the plane and walked into the huge airport.

My heart was beating so loudly I thought other people could hear it as we stood in the line to get through Customs. It was all becoming real—my legs were shaking and my palms were sweaty as I waited to show the official my passport. I wasn't expecting to feel so intimidated, but I had built up visiting the U.S. in my head so much, and I was about to live in this incredible country I had dreamed about living in for so long.

After we all got through Customs and retrieved our luggage, we loaded up on a big bus to drive to our apartments. I remember looking out the window and seeing the giant four-lane highways with all the fancy cars going by and thinking that the U.S. was exactly what I thought it would be—a beautiful, rich country, brimming with opportunity.

The salon I worked at was right in the middle of the city, close to the Capitol building. My coworkers and I took the metro to work every day from our apartments, which were in Arlington, Virginia, about a 25-minute metro ride away from the salon. We also used the metro or taxis to get around everywhere else. I had recently secured my driver's license in France, but didn't have a chance to use it there. I discovered I didn't need it in D.C. either, living in the middle of the city with public transportation readily available.

I enjoyed working in that salon and the opportunity to learn more English—I could barely speak it when I moved to D.C., but the company supplied translators for us. Some of the other hairstylists could speak both French and English, so they would help those of us who couldn't speak English fluently.

We all worked Monday to Friday from 9-6, then Saturdays 9-4. It was a busy schedule, but I didn't mind at all. We received a little bit of training once we arrived, but all of us had our master cosmetologist degrees, so we were fairly competent. We were excited to cut American people's hair, and they were excited to have French-trained hairstylists cutting their hair. All of us in the program would hang out and get food together after work most nights, since we didn't know anyone else.

There weren't a lot of things that surprised me about life in the U.S., as France was pretty similar in the way that people lived. I do remember being awed by the big highways, roads and parking spaces. Most of the roads where I lived in France were only one-lane roads, and most of the parking spots were on the sides of the roads. I loved the convenience of drive-throughs; Big Macs at McDonald's became my favorite American food. Another amazing perk was air conditioning being the norm in every building and home.

Something strange to me I noticed among the throngs of people who would walk the streets of D.C. heading to work were the women dressed up in their business suits, but wearing tennis shoes and carrying their dress shoes. I remember seeing them and thinking, *wow, I still can't believe I'm actually in America.*

Even though I was excited for all these new opportunities, I continued to struggle with my self-confidence. I worried about being the youngest in the program and not speaking English well enough. I felt like the other hairstylists connected better with each other than with me. They could talk about more mature themes that I didn't understand, like dating and going out, since I was sheltered growing up.

I tried to find an apartment with another girl in the program before my two months were up in the company-owned rental. Unfortunately, that didn't work out, and I ended up finding a studio apartment for myself in downtown D.C. It was a quick subway ride into work, so it was a safe, convenient location for me to be, and as a bonus, I had a great view of the Washington Monument right from my bedroom window. It was furnished with a couch, a table, two chairs and a mattress laying on the floor. It wasn't amazing, but I was content having a place to call my own.

My apartment was in a fairly large building, complete with a swimming pool, gym and even a small supermarket. I exercised there, did my shopping there and discovered it was a great place to practice my English and meet more people. I tried to spend more time hanging out with Americans at that point than I did with my group from France so I could learn the culture and language quickly. I did get to meet some people from Morocco in my building, which was a sweet surprise.

Once I had settled in, my confidence began to soar. I was thriving and finally felt like I had found a place I belonged. I loved being independent and providing for myself, and I focused on living life to the fullest as I enjoyed all the new opportunities the U.S. had to offer.

I didn't go out into the city much, but when I did I went to clubs with coworkers or people I met in my apartment building to go dancing, which I still loved to do. I think it was in my blood from Morocco, since it was the only thing I was able to do for fun there. It made me feel so free and bold and still gave me the most peace I had ever felt at that point in my life.

One Saturday night about seven months after moving, I was out in Georgetown with some of my coworkers at a club to go dancing. I remember feeling so confident and beautiful that night, as I whirled around the dance floor with my friends. We were speaking French with each other, and that caught the attention of a group of guys who were hanging out at the bar.

They came over to talk to us, and one of them in particular wanted to get to know me.

His name was Garrett. He was tall and well-built, with sandy brown hair and light-colored eyes. One of my friends who spoke English much better than me helped me introduce myself and chat with him a little bit about my job and how I had come from France to work in D.C. I don't remember much of our conversation, except that we connected and ended up dancing together that night. I found out that Garrett and his buddies were in the Army, stationed at Joint Base Andrews in Maryland, and they had come up to D.C. to enjoy their weekend off-duty.

I did the best I could with my broken English and my friend translating, but as we talked that night I was intrigued by him and enjoying the attention. I remember feeling confused about why he was spending time talking with me, since I didn't feel like his equal as a foreigner who couldn't communicate with him very well. I also didn't really understand flirting at that point in my life after growing up around a family who rarely showed affection in public. I was only a naive 19-year-old, and he seemed to be a hotshot military man, even though he was only about a year older than me.

Before we left for the night, we exchanged phone numbers, and he said one thing before he left that shocked me.

"I'm going to marry you."

He was definitely joking, but looking into his eyes I couldn't tell if he was slightly serious. I laughed and said goodbye, but the words kept replaying in my head over and over again as I walked home. *Could this guy be the one?*

The whole time I had been in the U.S., my visit with the psychic in France kept popping into the back of my mind. I had kept an eye out for any man from the government, naively telling myself that my dream of marrying an American man and having a family was finally going to come true.

The next couple of months were exciting ones for me as we started dating. I dreamed more and more about how the life I wanted for so long might finally be coming together. We talked on the phone a few times, and I did the best I could to communicate. I talked to him on a payphone or the home phone in my apartment, as we didn't have cell phones back then. For one of our dates, he drove the hour up to D.C. to pick me up, took me back to his base to show me around the area, and took me to dinner.

A few months after we met, the ringing of my home phone woke me up at 4 a.m.—he called to tell me he was getting transferred to San Antonio, Texas. I remember his voice clearly on the line as he said, "Hey, I'm being sent to Texas, and I have to leave in a few days. If you want to see me again, you'll have to go with me, and the only way to go with me is if you marry me. So…would you marry me?"

I said yes.

It was crazy, but looking back on that younger version of myself, I have compassion for my impulsive decision. I was so naive and sheltered, since I didn't really have any experience with bigger social settings or how to flirt or talk to boys. I had just started going out on my own when I turned 18 in France and was still learning so much about how the world worked.

Having grown up under my grandmother's constant, belittling abuse, moving countries twice, never feeling good enough, always feeling like an outsider, never truly belonging anywhere—I was so ready to be loved. My soul craved acceptance from someone who saw me and loved me for who I was. Even having a loving mom, stepdad and sisters, I felt like I needed that validation from an outsider.

Later that day after he called to propose, I called my mom to tell her about Garrett, explained the situation and told her we were getting married. She was shocked and scared. "What?! No. You're not doing that. You don't know this guy." I tried to convince her, telling her what a nice guy he was and that we were going to have a great life together. She tried to warn me, but I shrugged off her words as coming from an overly cautious mother who loved me but didn't know what she was talking about. I wasn't going to let this opportunity to have my life-long dream pass me by.

I was scared to tell my boss about my decision, afraid that he would hold me to my contract or worse, send me back to France. I was already disappointed with the company and used that as an excuse in my head to not tell them.

A few months before, I was out with friends walking by the river in Georgetown. It was late, we had already been to the club and decided to walk around a little before we all headed home for the night. We passed a restaurant that was surrounded by divider ropes separating the entrance from the walkway, and I made a stupid comment about how I could jump over them. My friends didn't believe I could, which made my competitive side flare up. I was wearing bell-bottomed pants and six-inch platform heels, so when I went to jump, the heel on my back foot caught the rope and I fell hard, twisting my ankle so badly I couldn't even stand up.

Thankfully, there was an American guy with us who picked me up and took me to the hospital. It turned out I had a very badly sprained ankle, and was put in a cast and given crutches to use for six weeks. I called my boss, because my contract said the company was going to take care of my medical needs if I got injured. I told him I couldn't work for six weeks since I was on crutches, and asked for help with my rent since I wouldn't be getting paid. He said "I'm sorry, I can't help you," and hung up the phone.

I called my parents in a panic and begged my stepdad to help me, which of course he did. He bailed me out and sent $600 to cover my rent for those six weeks, but the whole experience put a sour taste in my mouth for the company. I felt like they could care less about me, and so I wasn't going to care about them. Now, looking back, I am grateful they gave me the chance of a lifetime by bringing me to the U.S. If it wasn't for them, I wouldn't be here.

So, being the foolish nineteen year-old I was, I told a few friends my plans, packed up my suitcase, and a few days later left D.C. with Garrett to start our new life together.

Chapter 9

When Dreams Go Dark

You did not choose me, but I chose you and appointed you so that you might go and bear fruit—fruit that will last— and so that whatever you ask in my name the Father will give you. —John 15:16

Our first stop once we left D.C. was Little Rock, Arkansas, where Garrett was from. We drove through the night from D.C. to the hospital where his dad worked as an X-ray tech. Garrett had explained to me that we had to get married quickly so we could get to his base in Texas, but promised me we would have a real wedding later.

I was disappointed that I wasn't going to get to wear a white dress and walk down the aisle for a traditional wedding, but I understood the situation. I was excited to marry him and start a life with him, but also sad because it wasn't happening the way I thought it should. I couldn't explain that to him fully in my broken English, so I tried to let it go. His dad married us right there in the hospital x-ray room when we arrived, and then we stayed at his dad's house for a few days before continuing on to San Antonio.

Garrett's parents were divorced, so we stopped by his mom's house to visit her as well. Part of my whole life dream of getting married, having two children and making a wonderful life together had always been the importance of family. I had wanted my husband to have parents who were together, so I didn't have to add any more brokenness to my family. This was another disappointment for me with Garrett, but I pushed past it, since his parents were kind and I had already decided he was the answer to my lifelong dream.

The only other place I remember going while we were in Arkansas was the courthouse to get all our official paperwork finalized. I'm not sure how we were able to do everything, since all I had was my French driver's license—my passport had been stolen along with my wallet and all my cash while I was living in D.C. Somehow, we were still able to get officially married and get my military ID. He got me a ring from a pawnshop, and that was it—we were married.

At the time, I wasn't concerned about any of the red flags—leaving my job, getting my passport stolen, only knowing him for a couple months before getting married, him coming from a broken family, or not having the wedding I wanted. I was in the zone with Garrett, and nothing could faze me.

I was able to buy calling cards to check in with my parents and update them on my life. My mom still wasn't thrilled, but she knew she couldn't have done anything more to stop me. Garrett was never interested in talking with them on the phone, and it would've been difficult because of the language barrier. I didn't really care, since that meant I could use all the time catching up with them—I missed them so much, but was also so happy to finally be living my dream life in America.

Once we arrived in Texas, we lived in a small two-story apartment just off the base. Thankfully, it was already furnished, since neither one of us had many possessions. Garrett helped me find a job at the nearby hair salon at Fort Sam Houston, so I was able to get to work quickly. He was in school there to be an assistant dentist for the military and wasn't making much money, so we needed my income as well. But I didn't mind, and I wanted to stay busy during the days while he was gone. I started settling into a comfortable routine of life working, making meals and cleaning the apartment. We went out with some of his friends a few times, but mostly stayed at home together.

After a few months, I started feeling some discontent with our relationship. Garrett didn't seem as interested in me as he was when we first met, and he never brought up planning for our real wedding. He stopped initiating conversations, and seemed annoyed when I would try to talk about it. He was not romantic towards me at all, and I was starting to think this wasn't the life I had imagined for myself.

I remember one specific day we were arguing, and I finally brought up how I was feeling. He didn't seem to understand and got very upset at me. I got upset too, and was having a hard time expressing myself since I was still working on my English. I kept trying to explain, because I so badly wanted him to understand and start loving me the way I had longed to be loved for so long.

That was the first time he slapped me.

Smack!

I remember the hard sting I felt as his hand connected with my face. Tears sprang to my eyes. I quickly blinked them back, feeling numb as I tried to grasp what had just happened. I was so surprised; I didn't know how to act or what to say. My mind was racing... *What just happened? What is going on?* I shut down and walked away in shock, afraid to voice what had just happened.

The next time we argued, the same thing happened again, then again and again. Finally, I got up the courage to ask Garrett why he was hitting me. He was so apologetic: "I'm sorry, Karima, I'm so so sorry. I'm just stressed out, there's a lot going on at work and I'm just under a lot of pressure right now." He explained that he was getting transferred again, this time to Alabama for a more permanent position. He promised that once we got there, everything would be different and better for us. My English still wasn't great, and I didn't want to argue, so I accepted his excuse and tried to be the best wife I could be to him.

I began feeling stressed and anxious, wondering why my marriage was turning dark so quickly. One day at work, after the abuse had happened several times, I remember taking a smoke break at the salon—I started smoking cigarettes right before I left France—to try to quiet my mind and get rid of some of the stress I was feeling. I was leaning against the building, lost in thought, when a woman walked past me, stopped, turned and said, "God loves you," and walked away.

That was weird, I thought, as I watched her disappear down the street. Garrett had told me many times that he didn't believe in God, which didn't bother me since my faith was nonexistent. We didn't go to church, and the thought that Allah even thought about me, let alone *loved me* was so ridiculous I didn't give what she said a second thought. I was too busy trying to deal with my problems the best way I knew how, trying to figure out how to be a better wife to Garrett so that he wouldn't feel so much pressure.

Thinking back to that time, I remember how desperately I wanted our marriage to work. I thought I had found my dream man, my life, my answer. Divorce was not a thought that ever crossed my mind, since all I craved was a whole, loving family. I felt there must be something wrong with me, that I was flawed at some deep level and it had affected every environment in my past—so why should I believe this situation with Garrett was any different? He was sorry, so sorry, and he apologized profusely every time after he hit me. I clung to the hope that once we moved, things would change—that *he* would change—and somehow become the loving husband I had been longing for my whole life.

Chapter 10

Sworn to Silence

"I will be a Father to you, and you will be my sons and daughters," says the Lord Almighty. —2 Corinthians 6:18

That December, we moved to Fort Rucker, Alabama (now known as Fort Novosel). In one short year, my life had changed so much—coming over from France, working in D.C., marrying Garrett, moving to Texas and now living in Alabama. There, we lived in a small house on the base, in a neighborhood that felt like a little village. It had a place to buy groceries, a post office, a gym—all the basics were covered. I got a job at a barbershop off the base this time, but it was very close, so I still did a lot of military haircuts. I connected with a few of the other wives on base but didn't form any close friendships.

My funniest language mistake happened at that shop while I was still learning basic English. I was cutting a young guy's hair one day, and I commented that his eyebrows really needed to be trimmed. He was very insistent that he didn't want his eyebrows trimmed, until finally I put my fingers by his sideburns to show him how badly his "eyebrows" needed a trim. We had a good laugh once he explained the difference between sideburns and eyebrows, and I was very apologetic as I trimmed his sideburns.

Alabama was a different world from D.C. It surprised me to realize the U.S. actually did have poor people. Living in D.C., I only noticed government workers or people who, in my mind, looked like they belonged in the prosperous U.S. I had seen on TV when I lived in France.

I got my first car shortly after we moved—it made life much more convenient with us working our separate jobs. Garrett drove me to and from work when we were in Texas, but by the time we moved I was familiar with the U.S. roads and signs and felt comfortable driving myself. I remember us going to the DMV for me to get my U.S. license—they had me take a written test to make sure I knew all the signs and rules of the road.

After I finished, the gentleman helping me just looked at me and asked, "Do you remember how to drive?" *I just got my license in France and came straight here…I don't have that much experience.* "Yeah, I remember how to drive," I said, feigning confidence.

In order to get my license in France, I had spent about 30 hours in the car with a driving instructor and taken a written test as well. I had learned on a little manual car in the hilly French countryside, so I hoped it would come back to me quickly. Thankfully, he gave me my U.S. license right then and there without making me actually drive for him.

My first car was a very old, little manual—we didn't have extra money to spend on a nicer car. I had always wanted a sports car, so after I started making more money at my job I upgraded to a brand new, teal-green Mustang. It wasn't the smartest financial decision; we had a 14% interest rate on it since Garrett didn't have great credit and I had none at all, but I loved riding around in that car. Eventually, I traded that in and got an older red Camaro that I kept for a long time.

Our life was fairly normal for a short while—we would

take turns cooking meals, I would clean, and he would do little projects around the house, since he was pretty handy with tools. I was so hopeful that once we settled in, things would be different between us and we would grow closer. Instead, our relationship went from bad to worse.

The slaps escalated to pushes and shoves, and eventually to him putting his hand over my throat, trapping me against the wall with his body and choking me. He called me names on a daily basis, telling me straight to my face that I was ugly, skinny and worthless. He never injured me to the point I would bruise or have any marks; he was careful to limit his abuse to things that only left permanent marks on my soul.

As months passed, I continued to ask him why he was treating me this way. I remember saying, "Why are you doing this to me? What have I done to you? I work, I clean the house, I'm kind to you—what am I doing wrong that makes you so upset at me?" Every time I asked, he would apologize and sometimes even cry. "I'm so sorry Karima, I'm so sorry." He always had some sort of excuse, and I would leave those conversations feeling bad for him, guilty that I wasn't doing more to help him deal with whatever stress was causing him to lash out. I always convinced myself to believe he was sincere, until the next time it happened.

At first, it didn't seem like that big of a deal since he was apologizing so often. I kept telling myself, *Karima, this is still better. You're married, you have a roof over your head, a vehicle and a job—it's going to be okay.* I was only able to delude myself for so long.

On top of the physical abuse, he became extremely controlling. He didn't want to show me attention or love or care, but also didn't want me finding any of that anywhere else. He would pick what I could or couldn't wear and would call my work multiple times every day to make sure I was still there. We didn't go out much, and when I went out alone he controlled when I left and told me when I should be back. When I went to the commissary to buy groceries, I would get so scared that I would see a customer from the salon who would want to talk to me, because I knew he would be furious if he saw me talking to another man. I started regretting coming to the U.S., and kept asking myself, *how did I get here?* I felt so lost and rejected once again.

When I would get home from work, instead of being greeted with a "Hey honey, how was your day?", he would immediately question me: "Where the f*** have you been?! You're fifteen minutes late, what have you been doing?!" I would try to explain that hair salons didn't have a set quitting time—if a customer came in five minutes before closing time, I still had to take them. That explanation would only earn me a slap or a shove, so I started just saying that I was sorry and that I had to work late to try to get away from him.

We got to the point where we were arguing every day—it was hell on earth. I volunteered to work extra hours just to get away from him. The shop I worked at was run by a lady who was so consumed with her business that she didn't pay any attention to me and let me work as much as I wanted. She was driven to increase her profits and was pushy about having us work late and take every customer. I was self-employed at the time, renting a chair in her salon and paying her a percentage of what I made. In a regular week, I worked 6 days, 10-12 hours each day.

Waves of fear would wash over me at the sound of Garrett's voice, or even thinking about his anger about something I had done. I started remembering Morocco more often; I felt like I was that helpless little girl wandering the souk all over again, terrified of seeing my grandmother and of feeling the physical and emotional sting of her constant disappointment and rejection.

During that first year after we moved, I got home from work one day and Garrett wasn't home. His car was in the driveway, so I looked all over the house but couldn't find him. All the houses on the base were very close together, almost on top of each other. There were houses right next door to us, but then there was another row of houses right behind our house too. I went outside, looking all around our house, and that's when I saw him.

He was in the house directly behind us, sitting on the floor. As I looked through the window, I could see another person, a woman. He was in there, sitting on the floor, painting our married neighbor's nails. I stood there in shock for a second, trying to rationalize in my head what was going on, and then walked directly into her house. I expected him to be surprised and upset to see me, but he calmly looked up at me, and said, "Hey. There's nothing happening, I just had some time since I came home early so I came over to check on Amber."

My mind was racing... *What in the world is this guy doing? How does he think this is okay?* The whole situation was so strange, it caught me completely off guard. My English had improved, but I still didn't speak well enough yet to be able to defend myself or explain what I was thinking. After that, I began feeling hopeless, realizing that maybe I couldn't be enough for whatever Garrett needed in a wife.

All of this led me into such a dark, depressed place. Divorce was still not crossing my mind as an option. I desperately didn't want to make the same mistakes as my mom, but somehow I had found my way into a horrible, abusive marriage. I didn't speak the language fluently until a few years after we moved, didn't have any family in the country and couldn't ever see them; I felt so alone—trapped, like I was on a deserted island. Somehow, I was in yet another situation where I felt like I didn't belong, wasn't good enough and couldn't do anything to fix it.

As the years passed, the abuse became the entirety of the relationship I had with Garrett. There was no conversation, no hanging out, no affection. I truly felt like I was living with a roommate—as a matter of fact, I think I would've had more of a relationship with a roommate than I had with him.

If I tried to sit on the couch with him, he would tell me to get up and sit somewhere else. He was either apathetic toward me or yelling at me, there was no in between with him. We would argue constantly, and I would threaten to leave almost daily, even though at the time I never meant it. When I would say that, he would shout right back, "You're not going anywhere! If you do, I'm going to kill you!"

I never wanted to call the cops when things got bad, because in my heart somehow I still loved him and had hope that things could change. I also knew he could get in a lot of trouble with the military if he was arrested. It never dawned on me that I had any power to leave or make any changes.

I called my family once a week, since it cost $20 for a 10-minute calling card. We didn't have Skype or Zoom at the time, so those conversations were the only connection I had to them. They would ask me how I was doing, and since I didn't want to terrify them I always lied and said things were good. Since they couldn't see me, they never suspected anything was wrong. I also wrote letters, and my stepdad would write back for the family. Since calling cards were so expensive, my mom would record herself on tapes and send them to me, and I would send her back tapes of me talking to her. Those tapes and conversations were like tiny sparks of light in my very dark life.

Eventually, I got to the point where I was crying myself to sleep every night. I couldn't eat, and I would throw up brown acid from being so upset, anxious and stressed. We fought every day. I had horrible migraines, so bad I wanted to bang my head against the wall. I lost weight, shriveling down to 90 pounds. I started drinking to calm myself down and find some type of comfort, and it also helped me fall asleep. Garrett had introduced me to champagne when we got married, which was the first time I had alcohol. I passed a little liquor store on my way home from work, and several nights a week I stopped and bought a little bottle to drink every night. I would sit on the couch, cry, drink, smoke a cigarette and wonder *how did I even get here? I used to be so healthy and full of life—what has happened to me?*

I didn't have any friends, and none of my family was in the country. Looking back, I think that season of life was even tougher than life in Morocco. By then, I had been failed by every single important person in my life, now even by my husband. It hurts so much when the people who are supposed to love you the most completely reject you. I felt like trash, completely worthless.

During that season of my life when I felt so alone, I would write. I let all my pain out on the thousands of pages in my journals. I wrote in French since I couldn't write in English very well, detailing everything Garrett did and said to me to get it off my chest. I didn't feel like I could talk to anyone without getting Garrett in trouble, so writing helped me get some of my bottled up emotions out.

Chapter 11

A Tiny Little Thing

If we confess our sins, He is faithful and righteous to forgive us our sins and to cleanse us from all unrighteousness. —1 John 1:9

By 1996, three years into our marriage, I was stuck in the same cycle—working, crying, throwing up, drinking and repeat. One morning, I woke up to the smell of Garrett's morning coffee, and literally almost threw up in my bed, the odor was so nauseating. I thought, *that's weird, normally I throw up at night.* I didn't think any more of it as I dragged myself out of bed to get ready for work.

I was chatting with a coworker later that day and casually mentioned my strange experience that morning. She turned and looked at me with a raised eyebrow and a smile, and said, "Hey, you might be pregnant." I laughed nervously and said, "No, there's no way." She shrugged and we went on with our day, but what she said burned a hole in my mind and formed a pit in my stomach.

There's no way, I kept thinking, over and over. I had been on the pill since I was 18 for my cycle, but other than when my mom took me to the doctor to get that prescription, we never talked about anything related to my sexual health. I knew nothing about cycles or pregnancy or anything. Soon after Garrett and I had gotten married, I learned there could be negative side effects to the pill, so I had stopped taking it and was getting a shot every three months instead. Our intimacy had dwindled to almost nothing, so I didn't think pregnancy was even a possibility.

Since there were no tests you could buy in the store at that time, I went to the military hospital that afternoon. I couldn't wait any longer, because I couldn't stop thinking about it.

When the nurse came back into the room after running the test, she was smiling from ear to ear. "You're pregnant! Are you excited?"

My stomach felt like it hit the floor. Her voice slowed into an echo, and I felt like I was in a dream as I leaned back in my chair, gripping the arm rests with my fingers until my knuckles turned white. *No, no, no!* My thoughts were screaming. *This can't be happening. No!*

She could tell I was upset, and offered to do a blood test to confirm the results for sure. I remember her saying, "If this is positive, there's no denying it." I sat and waited anxiously for what felt like hours for her to come back. Finally, she came back and confirmed: "I'm sorry, it's positive. You are 4-6 weeks pregnant." My heart sank.

My stomach was churning as I drove home from the hospital and the reality of my situation started hitting me. I couldn't believe that instead of starting my dream life, I was going to be bringing a child into the same horrific cycle of abuse that I was brought into. I would be doing to this child what was done to me—bringing them into a broken, abusive family. I couldn't even wrap my mind around it.

When Garrett got home, I told him right away. I was always honest with him and never kept anything from him, and thought *why should I start keeping things from him now*? I figured he would find out anyway. I also had a shred of hope that maybe somehow this baby could bring us together. He seemed shocked when I told him, but then the first words out of his mouth were, "You're not having this baby."

At that time, I didn't even know what abortion was. I had never heard of it and didn't know it existed. I had been trying to come to terms with the fact that I was going to have a baby with this man and be abused together with his baby now. So, when those words came out of his mouth, I was so confused.

"What do you mean? It's already here, in my belly," I said.

"There's a place we're going to go, and I'll take you there," he said, almost gently. "Because the baby is so tiny, they can just take it out. It's not a big deal."

My mind was spinning as he kept explaining, reminding me that we didn't have a lot of money, and that we were so young. I remember him saying he wasn't ready to have a baby. I brought up his plan with a few of my coworkers, and they didn't seem surprised. They also reassured me it would be no big deal, that the whole process would be quick and easy. I remember one of them saying, "It's a piece of rice, and it doesn't even have a heartbeat. If you do this, it'll be nothing. It's just a tiny little thing, so they just pull it out so it doesn't grow, and that's it." I remember they did tell me to be careful in case there were people outside the clinic trying to convince me not to go in—they said not to listen to them.

I was terrified as we drove to the clinic in Birmingham a few days later. I didn't know how to feel or what to expect, just that everyone I told said it was "no big deal." I didn't have Google or any way to try to learn more about what Garrett was having me do. Part of me felt so sick about it, but I also knew it would do no good to resist him. And I so badly didn't want this child to grow up in the same type of abuse and brokenness that I did.

We walked in, Garrett signed me in, and a nurse took me back all by myself right away. She was very chatty and almost lighthearted, telling me the same thing my friends did: that "it" was just a tiny, tiny speck, and the procedure was not a big deal at all. She said, "We're gonna pull it out, and bam. You're done."

That's all the explanation I got of what was going on. I had never felt so young, confused, scared and alone than at that moment. She handed me a pill and told me to swallow it. Then, she had me lay down on a table and put my feet up on a stand. I couldn't see her any more, and she didn't say anything else as she leaned in to start.

That's when I felt the pain—it was like someone was tearing my insides out. I started throwing up almost immediately. The whole thing took a few minutes, but it was some of the most awful pain of my life. I was in tears when she was finished.

She had me get up almost immediately, gave me a pad and sent me back out to Garrett. He paid and then we left. We had to stop a few times on the way home for me to throw up, and I couldn't stop crying the whole way back.

I was sick for several days, not only physically but also mentally, as I tried to block out what had just happened. I didn't know how to feel—I wasn't religious in any way at this point, besides just trying to be a good person, and Allah was the furthest thing from my mind. Part of me was relieved I wasn't going to have a baby with Garrett. There would be no child for him to abuse.

But another part of me ached so badly for this baby I would never hold, never get to love. For years, I had moments where I thought randomly, *oh my gosh, my baby would be five years old now.* I wondered whether it was a boy or a girl. Every time I saw a baby, I thought about *my* baby, and my body almost physically hurt missing this person I had never met. That choice haunted me for a long, long time.

Chapter 12

Resident Alien

Consequently, you are no longer foreigners and strangers, but fellow citizens with God's people and also members of his household. —Ephesians 2:19

My health continued to decline, and Garrett continued to ignore me. Nothing in my day-to-day life changed, and I continued to sink deeper and deeper into depression, yet hoping that somehow after I went through the abortion that he would have some sympathy for me. That was too much to hope for.

In November 1996, the same year as my abortion, one day my body finally said ENOUGH. I was working at the salon like every other day, and all of a sudden I felt my heartbeat speed up and begin pounding in my chest. I could feel it vibrating all over my body. Thinking I just needed a break, I stepped outside for a smoke, but it didn't stop, and kept getting faster and louder.

I went back inside after my cigarette since I had another customer in my chair, but I started feeling lightheaded and nauseous. I briefly explained what was going on to my customer, who immediately said, "You need to go to the hospital. Come on, I'll drive you."

My thoughts were racing, but the first one that crossed my mind was that if Garrett somehow saw me in the car with this guy, he'd kill me. But I started to freak out and didn't have anyone else who could take me, so I went with him. After he dropped me off at the emergency room, I went in and told the girl at the front desk that my heart was beating very fast and I needed help. She took my pulse right there, and cussed when she saw the number: 250. She called back to her coworker and said, "We need to take this lady back right away!"

They put me in a bed and got me back to a room very quickly, and a doctor started me on an IV with medication to slow down my heart rate, but it didn't slow down. He explained that to fix what was going on, they were going to have to stop my heart and restart it. I was scared out of my mind at this point, and my heart was pounding in my ears. I didn't have a cell phone, so I couldn't call Garrett quickly to tell him what was happening, it was all happening so fast.

I watched the doctor use a syringe to push the medicine into my IV. As soon as it entered my body, I could feel it creeping up my arm into my shoulder, into my neck and head and down into my chest. I felt immense pressure, like someone was sitting on my chest. I gasped for air, choking. Those couple of seconds felt like long minutes before I could finally get a breath, once my heart restarted.

That day was my wake up call. I finally realized the toll my lifestyle was taking on my body. I remembered being so proud of how strong I was just a few short years before, and there I was a weak shell of that woman. I was still in my early 20s, but felt like I was 60. I remember thinking, *if I don't leave this marriage, I'm going to die. Garrett is either going to kill me, or I'm going to die.*

Garrett came to take me home later that day and didn't seem too concerned when I told him what happened. However, the doctor was concerned, so I had to go in the next week for a follow-up appointment. I went alone, and he asked me several questions to see how I was recovering. He told me it looked like I had some type of panic attack, and asked, "Is everything at home okay?"

Here was a chance literally presenting itself to me, where I could've gotten help so easily. But I quickly lied and said, "Yes, of course! Everything's fine." He asked me if I was sure—I think he could sense something was off about me. I smiled and reassured him that I was completely fine. He tried to prescribe me an anti-anxiety medication, but since I had never been a fan of taking any medicine, I told him I would be fine, thanked him and walked out of the hospital.

After I recovered from that incident, I finally considered what it would mean to leave Garrett. The more I thought about it, the more I thought I had to try just one more thing to get his attention. I had an idea that had been in the back of my head ever since I had initially lost most of my weight and gotten down to 90 pounds—breast implants.

Because I had lost so much weight, I had also gone down a breast size, so I thought maybe, as my last shred of hope, I would get implants and see if he would give me any attention then. I convinced myself that I just needed to make my body better for him in this way. I asked some of my coworkers about it, and found out that I could actually get the procedure done in the hospital on the Army base I lived in.

I asked Garrett about it, and he was fine with me doing it; he didn't seem to care either way. I went to see the surgeon, who told me the procedure was very easy. He would just cut a small incision underneath each breast and put the implants in underneath the muscle. He said the implants themselves were just a silicone shell filled with saline water, so they were no danger to me, and if they ruptured, they would simply deflate.

All I had to pay was $500 for the implants themselves, and my health insurance would cover the surgery. I remember feeling very excited, thinking about how easy this was to just fall asleep and wake up with bigger breasts. I didn't really think about the possibility of future complications, it just felt good to be doing something that I thought would help my self-esteem and my marriage.

When I woke up after the surgery, it felt like an elephant was sitting on my chest. The pressure and pain were uncomfortable, but the surgeon told me it went well, and gave me some pain medication for the next few days. Garrett took me home that day, and I recovered quickly and was up and back to work within a week. I remember looking in the mirror and being so pleased with how my body looked, and couldn't wait for Garrett to notice or say something about them. He never did.

As the weeks passed, I realized that nothing I did would make a difference with him, and I felt like I had hit rock bottom. Later that year, a woman came to me and told me that Garrett had cheated on me with her. She didn't come to me in a vindictive way to try to steal him away—I think she was just trying to let me know what kind of man he was, in case I didn't know. I told her I didn't believe her, but deep down I did.

Earlier that year, I had decided I was finally going to go back to France to see my family. I told Garrett that I was going, and surprisingly he didn't say no. We bought tickets to go to France for Christmas 1997, and then tickets to visit Morocco after that. It was a long, expensive trip, but I was so ecstatic to see my family again after three years.

Because we had a trip planned, I needed to get my passport replaced. I had never bothered to get a new one since mine had been stolen back in D.C. since I hadn't needed it. Garrett and I took a day off work and he drove me to the closest passport office, which was several hours away in Atlanta, Georgia. When I got there and explained my situation, the lady said she needed proof that I had a French passport. I tried to explain that I didn't have any proof, which is why I needed help. She said "I'm sorry, I can't help you," and moved on to the next person.

Panicked, I called my stepdad. I begged him to help me—I was terrified that I would be stuck away from my family forever. Thankfully, he was able to call the embassy in Paris, where I got my first passport, and they had all my initial paperwork. They were able to send all of that to the office in Atlanta, so we drove back the next day. I was able to get my new French passport and green card, officially labeling me as a "resident alien" in the United States—yet another label to remind me I didn't belong anywhere.

Our trip for Christmas that year was such a highlight for me. When I had left France, my little sisters were three and five; now they were six and eight. For some reason I thought time would stand still there until I got back, and I was surprised to see how grown up they were.

Even though I was lying to them about my marriage, it was so good seeing my family again. It was especially life-giving to get to see my mom—our reunion was very emotional. It felt like those times as a little girl when she visited me in Morocco once a year—I just wanted to drink her in. Garrett was nice to my family, and they didn't suspect anything was wrong. I always put a smile on my face, even though I was hurting inside. I never showed anyone how bad it was—I didn't want anyone to know what was happening or to think badly of him.

After we spent a week or so in France, Garrett and I flew to Morocco with my mom and sisters. We were upstairs alone one day and during a disagreement he shoved me down to the floor and started choking me. I remember gasping for air when he finally let me up, tears stinging the corners of my eyes. I was angry and scared at the same time, shocked that he would do that while we were in the same house as my family. I had thought there was no way he would put his hands on me while we were on this trip, but I was wrong.

I walked downstairs, and just so happened to run into my mom right away. She could tell something was wrong by my red face and tear streaks around my eyes, and immediately asked me, "Karima, what's wrong?"

"Nothing, I'm fine," I lied. I couldn't let her know what I was going through—I knew it would cause her so much pain, and I wanted to keep protecting her from that. I knew she already worried about me being so far away. But she wouldn't let it go. "I can tell something's wrong," she said. "Tell me what happened."

Finally, I broke down, and everything came pouring out like a tidal wave. I finally had someone to talk to. What I didn't realize at the time was that I had always had someone to talk to. I couldn't hide it from her any more, and I told her everything.

That was when I found out about my dad's abuse of my mom. I never knew that part of the story, just that he gave me up and died young. Once I had calmed down, she said,

"Let me tell you what happened with your dad." I was able to empathize with my mom on a whole other level that day. She had always been my best friend, but that day we connected like never before. Of course, she was livid with Garrett and said, "He needs to leave right now." It felt so good to finally have someone know and be on my side. We made up a story to tell my grandmother, that he had an unexpected death in his family and had to leave in a hurry, because we knew how angry she would be if she found out what was really going on. For all her flaws, she was fiercely protective of her family from outsiders.

I told Garrett that my mom knew what had happened and that he needed to leave. He got emotional and kept apologizing, like usual, but he knew if he resisted things could get bad with my family, especially with my grandmother. We sent him back to France, where my stepdad met him at the airport, helped him pack up his stuff and put him on a plane back to the U.S. a few days later.

I remember feeling so relieved that last ten days with my family. I didn't have to be worried about arguing with him, upsetting him, or being abused—he was a whole ocean away, and I could just focus on filling myself up with precious time with my family.

From that time on, my mom told me many times that I could not stay in a relationship with him, and that I needed to leave him and come back home. She tried to convince me to stay in France with them and not go back at all. I didn't feel like I could do that to him or just leave my job, but I did seriously consider it. I felt like I left my body, and was floating above myself, looking at my life. Ever since I was a little girl, I had wanted to move to the U.S., marry the man of my dreams, have a boy and a girl with him and start a loving family. But my dream was falling apart, and I realized I was actually living a nightmare.

My heart ached as I grappled with the fact that he would never be the loving husband I wanted. After I got home from the trip and nothing changed with him, I finally accepted there wasn't anything I could do to change him or how he treated me. I had known it in my head for a long time, but it finally got down to my heart.

Many times during those years with Garrett in Alabama, I'd be driving to work and just think *I just want to hit that tree. I just want to be done. I just want to hit that tree and be done.* But I always talked myself out of it.

The thought that always stopped me from ending it all during that season of life was my mom. Every time I thought about quitting my life because I was so hopeless and my life was so horrible, I thought about how heartbroken she would be. How heartbroken my sisters, my step dad, my aunts and uncles would be—and that's ultimately what kept me from not doing it.

The suicidal thoughts came more times than I could count, mostly when I was alone in the quiet of my car driving to work. Part of it was that I wanted attention from Garrett. I remember thinking *maybe if I really hurt myself, he'd notice me.* I had given up on his love, coming to terms with the fact that maybe I didn't deserve to be loved by anyone.

Later that year, I vividly remember one of those lonely nights crying in front of the TV. As I was flipping through the channels sipping my evening drink, I found one where someone was preaching. Although I can't recall what he said, his words felt hopeful, so I kept watching.

RESIDENT ALIEN | 87

At the end, the guy said, "Bow your head and pray with me," so I did. I didn't even know what I was doing—it was like my body was moving without me in control. I remember thinking, *there's got to be more to life than what I'm living now.* I felt worthless and unlovable, and even though customers at my shop would tell me I was beautiful on a daily basis, it didn't matter, because I went home and the only person I cared about hearing those words from put me down. The little confidence I had built by the time I met Garrett had evaporated under his harsh treatment, and I was desperate for real love.

When I heard that sermon and bowed my head with that TV preacher, tears streaming down my face, something happened to me. I don't know what it was, and I didn't understand it at the time. Now I know—it was the first real seed of faith planted.

Chapter 13

Gone for Good

Surely he will save you from the fowler's snare and from the deadly pestilence. He will cover you with his feathers, and under his wings you will find refuge; his faithfulness will be your shield and rampart. —Psalm 91:3-4

By early 1998, I had been seriously thinking about leaving Garrett for several months. I felt like I had tried everything I could possibly try, done everything I could do, and realized how much of a toll our marriage had taken on my body. I heard clients at the barbershop talk about their marriages, or about going through a divorce, and I remember thinking, *wait a minute, I'm not the only one going through this stuff. Maybe I do actually have a choice to get out of this. This way of living is not normal or okay.* I began to understand that divorce was more common than I had thought.

I remember sitting down one day and thinking about it—thinking through all five years of our marriage and everything that had happened. How time after time he had failed me. As each instance replayed in my head, I could almost feel the scales falling from my eyes. I finally accepted the fact that my dream life was never going to happen with Garrett. I had forgiven him countless times, and he continually let me down.

Around the same time I was coming to grips with my decision to move on, we went to a party together at one of his friends' homes. Everyone was hanging out, drinking, playing games and having a good time. I was trying to make the most of a night out, and had gotten down on the floor to play Twister. For some reason, that made Garrett mad—he leaned down and whispered in my ear: "Let's go home, right now."

At that moment, I decided enough was enough. I looked back up at him, and said "No. I'm not going home. I'm staying here." I was done being commanded by him, and wanted to live my life and do what I wanted to do.

He didn't know what to say for a second—I think he was surprised by my sudden confidence and defiance. "Well, you can either come home with me or stay here, but I'm taking the car and going home right now," he said.

I snapped right back: "You go right ahead," and went back to my game. I didn't think he was actually going to go and strand me at this party. *Surely he's not going to leave me with all these people by myself.* But I had overestimated him yet again. By the time I finished playing and looked around for him, he was gone.

Thankfully, I was speaking English fluently by then, and I asked someone to take me home when the party was over. Garrett and I had a huge fight when I got home, but I was fully aware of who he was and how he had been controlling me. That night for the first time, I stood up to him and said, "If you hit me, I'm going to hit you right back. I'm not going to allow you to push me around anymore. I'm done!"

I don't think he believed me at first. I had threatened to leave so many times, he didn't realize that something was different this time. I got a recommendation for a divorce lawyer from someone at work, and contacted them the next week to start the process. It only took a few weeks to be done, since we didn't have any children or assets. I told the lawyer I didn't care about any of our things, I just wanted out, which made it a very simple divorce. We both had our own cars in our names that we kept, and I moved out as soon as I could to an apartment right off the base in Enterprise. As a single man, he was now required to live in the barracks on base.

Because I grew up with so little in terms of a loving family for the first part of my life, I have always valued relationships most in life. That is why I strove so hard to keep our marriage going. I believed I had no choice with him. I believed him when he told me I was nothing, but still desperately wanted us to work. I was brainwashed—I felt trapped with no way out, never realizing all the ways I could have reached out for help. I could have talked to someone, anyone, at any point in the five years I endured his abuse. I had the choice to leave earlier, and wish that I had. I just didn't see a way out at the time. The abuse blinded me to the truth, which was that people will treat you the way you allow them to treat you.

One day soon after we had separated, Garrett called me in a panic. "I need you to please come to the barracks, or I'm going to hurt myself." He made it sound very urgent on the phone, that he was going to do something serious to himself if I didn't come, so I went. He asked me to sit down once I got there, and he apologized for everything again, but this time giving me new reasons why. He said he grew up in an abusive home—that his dad was an alcoholic and he had been abused as a child and watched his mom be abused as well.

I realized as he was talking that he truly did want to have a good marriage, he just didn't know how. His dad was a horrible example of what a husband should be, divorcing his mom after she had been disabled in a car accident. I realized that in some twisted way, Garrett did love me—he just didn't know how to express it. But I had already given him countless opportunities to treat me differently and he hadn't. I wasn't about to believe that he was changed now.

During the divorce process, Garrett called me almost daily, begging me to give him another chance. I held my ground and would respond every time with "No Garrett, I'm done." He would immediately get angry, yelling something like, "Well you're a b**** anyway, and nobody wants you! You're ugly and worthless, and I'm going to have you deported by immigration!" I would hang up, making up my mind that his tactics to shame me into being with him weren't going to work any more.

He would also call and say, "Hey, I saw you at a certain place, what were you doing?" I was terrified that he was following me and that he would try to grab me, so I had two deadbolts and three locks on my apartment door.

When I was moved out and waiting for the divorce to finalize, I had my worst scare with Garrett. He showed up to a Fourth of July party I was at on the base, drunk and begging me to stay with him, causing a scene in front of the whole neighborhood when I said no.

He got right up in my face, screaming, "I'm going to deport your a**. They're going to send you back to France tomorrow."

My friends came out of the house, concerned for my safety— the whole situation was a nightmare. The next day, I went out and got a restraining order against him. Someone at the party that night had told me I should do something to protect myself after they saw how Garrett approached me. I told my lawyer the truth, that I was scared for my life, and told him about the constant calls, the following and all the locks on my door. I didn't want to get a restraining order against him, but I felt like I had to, to protect myself.

Garrett's commander contacted me after that, and I told him, "I don't wish Garrett any harm; I'm just trying to protect myself. I just want to be left alone." He was very understanding and kind about it all, assuring me that this wouldn't affect Garrett's military career.

Garrett stopped contacting me after that, and about a month later once our divorce was official in August of 1998, he got stationed in Germany. I never saw him again. I was so grateful to finally be free. He was gone for good.

In Alabama, at the Fort Rucker house. You can see my drink and cigarette nearby and the miserable look on my face, 1995.

Chapter 14

Moroccan Redneck

Take my yoke upon you and learn from me, for I am gentle and humble in heart, and you will find rest for your souls.
—Matthew 11:29

During the next couple of months, I settled into my routine of working during the day and hanging out with friends at night. I had left the first shop I worked at in Alabama while Garrett and I were still married, realizing it wasn't the best environment for me. I tried working at a regular salon in Enterprise after that, but it was so slow without all the military haircuts, and I was making much less money on tips.

By the time we got divorced, I was already at a different shop just outside the base called Mr. Ji's. The owner, a Korean man, hired me on the spot when I went in looking for a job. He and my coworkers were so kind, even coming up with an affectionate nickname for me. I had been trying to learn southern slang, and asked one of my coworkers what "y'all" meant. After that, I was jokingly known as the Moroccan redneck. I was much busier there than at my previous job, so it was a great move for me financially. Sometimes, the boss would bring in homemade egg rolls for all of us—he created a fun atmosphere to work in.

One day, someone came into the shop and asked if he could hand out little religious cards. Mr. Ji let him, and I took one out of curiosity before he left. It had a picture of a man on the front, with the words, "Jesus, I trust in you," and the back had a bunch of little sayings on it. I didn't understand it, but somehow it reminded me of the peace I found that night when I prayed on the couch when I was still married. I stuck it in my wallet and moved on.

On the weekends, I would hang out at clubs or parties with friends, doing whatever I wanted to do. I gained my weight back, and along with it more self-confidence. I realized how I had chosen to be trapped in Garrett's expectations and desires, and deliberately tried to not let other people's opinions or ideas affect my choices. I was still kind and respectful to people, but I was finally living my life however I wanted.

I still didn't have close friends at the time. There was one girl, Allie, who lived across the street from my apartment with her military boyfriend. After we met, they took me in and watched out for me while my divorce process was going on, which was amazing. I enjoyed hanging out with them and was so grateful for their protectiveness.

I had a few guys who expressed interest in me, but I wasn't interested in their attention. The first guy I started talking to after the divorce was Torin, who I met at a mutual friend's party. What drew me to him was his genuine kindness; he was just a very nice guy. We exchanged numbers and started going out together, but it always felt very casual, because neither of us were interested in any serious commitment at the time.

He was in military flight school, so when he graduated about a year after we started going out, he received transfer orders to be stationed in Savannah, Georgia. He asked me if I wanted to go with him, and I agreed, since I didn't have any other plans and knew I could find a job anywhere. I had so much pain from all the memories in Alabama that I was eager to move to a new place. We weren't serious in our relationship at this point, but I was still excited to start fresh and see where things went. One of his military friends already lived there, so we moved into his apartment initially. Soon after we moved, Torin bought his own house in Savannah and I moved with him there and paid rent.

I went out into the city to find work right after we moved. I vividly remember walking into the first salon. It was a warm day, and I had a long sundress on. I asked the girl at the front of the shop if they were hiring anyone, and she turned around and yelled toward the back, "Hey Tammy, we have someone asking for a position!"

A woman turned and walked up from the back. The first thing I noticed about her was that she had kind blue eyes, and as we made eye contact and she smiled, I could just tell she was a good boss. Before I could say a word, she said, "Okay, you're hired." I started working for her the next day and did very well there. It was another salon close to a military base, so the military traffic kept us bustling.

Once we settled in, Torin and I lived a pretty normal life—there was nothing really special about it. I lived my life and he lived his. We lived like single people who enjoyed hanging out with each other. He never told me what to do and didn't care what I did. I dressed however I wanted, smoked, drank, partied—I was free to make my own choices.

I started working out again, and Torin and I took a few trips together: we vacationed in Florida and I visited him in Arizona during his flight training course. Still, our relationship remained casual. He was nice to me, but content to just be hanging out, doing our own things. Even though I finally had my freedom and a nice guy, life still felt empty.

Torin's parents were also sweet people, but the longer we dated, the more they started hinting about us getting married. I remember them asking me about it, to which I responded that I didn't know. After that, I asked Torin about marriage for the first time, to see if he was interested. He was pretty noncommittal about it, saying, "Ah, Karima, I just don't think I'm ready to get married."

I started to realize that maybe this kind of life was all he wanted, and I began considering what *I* wanted. I'd wake up, go to work, come home, have a drink, hang out with friends, rinse and repeat. *Is this all there is?* I remember thinking, *I'm just wasting my life.* I'd see people out with their spouses and kids, and realized that a big part of me still wanted my dream—a loving husband and two kids. A family.

I asked him again a few more times about marriage over the next couple of months, and his response was always the same. Finally, I asked him if he saw a future for us together. He said, "Well, I mean, aren't we good like this?"

That's when I knew this life wasn't good enough for me. I didn't want to be a girlfriend for another ten years in hopes he would be ready to marry me one day. My perspective had changed since Garrett; I wasn't living my life based on other people's expectations or desires. I was living my life for Karima. I had decided I was going to take care of myself, because no one else in my life had done it so far.

I remember waking up one day when I was considering moving on from Torin, my thoughts circling in discontent:

What am I doing here? I feel so empty. This is not what I want. I don't want this kind of life. I didn't understand—I had my job, my sports car, money, freedom and a kind man. But it still wasn't enough.

I wasn't finding any satisfaction in religion. Torin and his parents were Catholic but only went to church on Christmas. He didn't care what I did for religion, so I had no spiritual guidance from him at all.

As I continued to reflect on my life over the next few months, I felt like it was just failure after failure after failure. Nothing I had hoped for had happened, and I knew now it wasn't going to be with Torin. After almost two years of dating, I put my foot down with him. I told him he needed to make a decision about marriage, or I was going to leave.

"Well, I'm just not ready," was his response, so I said "Okay. Well, when you are ready, let me know. I'm leaving."

That day I got a U-Haul, packed up my stuff, put everything in a storage unit and left. I rented a room from a friend at her house at first, since I didn't want to get an apartment in case he changed his mind and wanted me to come back. I figured if he really cared about me, he would pursue me.

A few months went by, and I never heard from him. I was sad, because I thought once I left he would change his mind and want to marry me. I remember thinking *wow, he really doesn't want to commit. I wasted so much time with him.*

I had been with two men now over the course of my eight years in the U.S. who were complete opposites—one who controlled my every move, and one who let me be completely free. And neither of those satisfied my inner desire for a loving family. I had always felt a little lost with Torin, like I was trying to find myself after Garrett. Now that I had neither, I felt directionless, like I was drifting aimlessly through life.

After I came to terms with the fact that Torin wasn't going to be calling me saying he was ready any time soon, I called my mom. "I think I want to come back home." I was done trying. I had visited my family earlier that year and was reminded again of how much I missed and loved them. I thought, *what's the point of living here in the U.S.? I'd rather just go home and live with my family and my mom again. At least I still have them.*

I began fleshing out my plan to move back to France. My mom started sending me French household and car magazines, so I could get an idea for the current cost of living there. I continued working for Tammy at her salon, planning to save up enough money to buy a car and put a down payment on an apartment once I moved back. My neighbors, Julie and Ray, loved and supported me as I worked to move back home. I was so grateful for their companionship during that time.

It felt good to have a goal to work toward as I set money aside, but I still felt like life had lost its purpose. I was living life doing whatever I wanted to do, but I had completely given up on my dream. I felt like the last seven years of my life had been a complete waste of my time, so I was done searching for a relationship and done with men. I remember coming to terms with the fact that marriage and kids just weren't going to be for me, and that I would be single for the rest of my life.

I had other dreams, like owning my own hair salon one day, but being a wife and having kids had always been number one, ever since I had been a little girl begging in the souk of Marrakech. For me to fully give that up was a big deal, but I felt like I had tried and failed too many times to keep trying.

Part of me was excited to move back to France. I missed my family and time spent with them, especially around the holidays. We still only had phone calls or letters to connect, so I was looking forward to being around them again and watching my sisters grow up. Even though my years in France were tough with school, I had so many good memories from finally being with my mom, and living there with family seemed like the better option compared to living my life alone in the U.S.

Chapter 15

Blue Eyes and Biceps

Trust in the LORD with all your heart and lean not on your own understanding;in all your ways submit to him, and he will make your paths straight. —Proverbs 3:5-6

After my divorce, something I added back into my life was working out. I had always enjoyed it as a teenager, and it made me feel more independent and strong as a woman. Since I hadn't taken care of my body at all during the five years of my marriage, it felt like another thing I could do just for myself.

That's why I found myself at the local Savannah YMCA one chilly evening in January of 2001. I was close to my savings goal to move back to France, so as I worked out, I was thinking about that and my future after my move.

I was almost finished with my hour-long workout, so I moved to the free weight room for my last two exercises. As I sat down on a bench in front of a mirror to do some bicep curls, a guy walked behind me who I had never seen.

I saw big, burly guys at the gym all the time showing off, but this guy stopped me dead in my tracks. I couldn't fight the urge to turn and stare as he walked away.

He was very tall, muscular and fit, wearing black shorts and a black tank top. As he turned to talk to one of his friends, I caught a glimpse of his deep blue eyes—he was the epitome of a handsome American man.

I knew I had never seen this guy in the gym before, and my mind was screaming, *Oh my gosh–who is that guy?! I have to know.*

My last exercise was at the tricep machine, and as I did my sets there, a gym employee started a friendly conversation with me. He was from Haiti and spoke French, which is how we had connected before. The handsome American walked by and heard us speaking French, stopped and asked, "Hey, is that French you're speaking?"

I couldn't believe he was talking to me, but I responded, "Yes, I'm actually from there."

"Oh, that's so cool. That's awesome," he said. He smiled, then walked away to continue his workout.

After that, my mind was made up. I wasn't leaving if there was even a chance I could talk to him again. I was going to stay until he noticed me! I was done with my workout, but kept going, switching to legs since I had just worked out my upper body.

I started working out my calves at a machine next to where he was. When I finished my set, my one leg cramped all of a sudden, and I let out a breath in pain, putting my hand on my calf and exclaiming, "Ooh, that hurts!" He turned his beautiful blue eyes straight on me and asked, "Are you alright? Want me to massage that for you?"

He was joking, but I was like *sure, yes, go right ahead!* Trying to seem modest, I replied, "No, I'm good, thanks." We didn't talk any more during his workout, and when I saw him leave and head to the locker room, I grabbed my stuff to go. I was exhausted from working out for almost two hours, and knew I couldn't keep going until he walked out since I didn't know how long he would be.

Just as I walked out of the gym area, he walked out of the locker room. Inside, I was like *yes, let's go!* We started small-talking and getting to know each other. Our conversation flowed so naturally, and he was so honest—he told me he was married before, divorced for about ten years and had two kids, right off the bat.

I found myself sharing that I had been married before as well and was recently divorced, and had been living in Savannah for just over a year. I found out he used to live in Alabama at the same time as me and had moved to Savannah a few years back.

We clicked—it was an instant connection right away. I didn't normally talk with men like that, sharing some of those personal details, but it felt totally normal to be talking about life with him. He asked me what I did, and when I told him I was a hair stylist, he asked for my work number, saying, "I'd love to come by and get a haircut sometime."

I gave him a note with my name and number on it, and we said goodbye—his friends had been waiting for him in the lobby this whole time as he was talking to me. I couldn't wait to see him again.

I called a good friend in the car on my way home and said, "Oh my gosh, you're not going to believe this—I met this guy. Oh, you should see this guy! He is beautiful, my heart was beating so fast." I had never felt like this before—it was a new, exciting feeling to be this interested in a guy.

The next day, I went back to the gym at the same time, and he was there again. We said hi and acknowledged each other, but didn't talk much that time. But after that, he just disappeared. I tried going to the gym at different times on different days but didn't see him again. I remember thinking *what in the world? Where is he? Why didn't he call me or come to the shop?* As the weeks passed, my disappointment grew, and I realized he must not have been interested in me. It never dawned on me that maybe he had just gotten a haircut and didn't need one for a while.

About a month later on a random Tuesday, I was coming back to work from lunch, preoccupied as I looked at my full book of appointments. I walked out to the waiting room to call the first one, and that's when I saw him.

There was my handsome American guy, sitting right there in my waiting room. I didn't remember his name when we met—it had gone in one ear and out the other when we were talking, so I didn't recognize it on my list of appointments. He hadn't seen me walk out, so I didn't say anything, turned around, and walked back to the coloring room to collect myself.

My thoughts were racing. *Oh my gosh, what is he doing here?!* I had told Tammy about him after I had met him, so when I saw her in the back I said, "He's here!" She could see how excited I was…I could feel myself getting warm and my heart rate rising.

Once I took a few deep breaths, I walked back out to the waiting room, trying to play it cool. Our eyes connected, and he stood up and smiled his beautiful smile at me. My heart almost stopped right then and there.

I remember trying to be so nonchalant as I greeted him, "Oh hi! How are you?" We exchanged pleasantries, and then he said he was my first appointment of the afternoon. I looked at my book so I wouldn't forget his name—Roger Burdette.

I was so nervous as I cut his hair. I don't even remember what I said, I was just trying to make small talk and keep the conversation flowing. Between meeting him and seeing him that day, I had switched cars, so I talked about that. I had always wanted an SUV, so I had traded in my Camaro for a Dodge Durango. We were talking about the Camaro, and he said that he used to own one. I told him I had gotten a new car, and he said, "Oh, well I'd love to see it if you have time to show me."

So, after I finished his haircut, I walked outside with him to the car. He walked around it, commenting on how nice it was. I thanked him, but didn't know what to say. I wanted to spend more time with him, but I also had to get back inside to my other appointments.

Suddenly, he looked over at me from where he was standing next to the car and said, "Hey, do you want to get lunch sometime?"

"No, I'm sorry, I can't." Lunch is the busiest time of day for hairstylists—I only got a half hour to eat and get back to work. I watched the disappointment wash over his face. Quickly, I said, "But I can do dinner!" His eyes lit up—"Oh yeah? When is a good day for you?"

"How about tonight?" I asked. He seemed a little surprised, but said that would work for him, and asked where I wanted to meet. I suggested we meet right there in the salon parking lot—I was trying to be wise since I didn't know him or if he was secretly crazy, and I didn't want to give him my home address quite yet. He said he could pick me up at 6:30, so I said, "See you then!" and went back inside to finish working for the day.

He picked me up in his BMW at 6:30 that evening and took me to dinner. It didn't take me long to realize that this man was the whole package. He was so kind, opening doors for me, pulling out my seat and even making sure I was walking on the inside of the sidewalk farther away from the street.

No man had ever treated me like that, prioritizing or protecting me or being romantic. I was blown away by this kind, genuine and stunningly handsome man.

We ended up talking for hours that evening, even driving to a Moroccan restaurant for dessert to continue our date. We talked about life, our kids, our pasts—I felt like I knew him and could tell him anything, and it was obvious he felt the same. He dropped me back off at my car around 11:30 that night, and as I drove home all I could think about was when I would see him again.

Ironically, the next day was Valentine's Day. I was busy working when someone delivered a beautiful bouquet of flowers for me, with a card that said, "Happy Valentine's Day, Roger." I was so excited, but realized I hadn't gotten him anything, and I decided I needed to show him how interested I really was.

Tammy gladly gave me a few hours off—she could tell there was something special going on with me and this guy. I went to the nearest florist and bought a big bouquet of flowers and drove to Roger's work. It was a big office building, as he was the vice president of a trucking company. Someone met me at the door of his building asking what I was there for, and I said I was delivering flowers for Roger Burdette. He offered to take them for me, thinking I was a delivery person. Later, I learned he was Roger's boss, which made the whole situation even more comical.

"No, no, you don't understand," I said. "I'm here to give him the flowers." He smiled and let me in, but said that Roger was busy at the moment, and I could have a seat in the waiting room until he was free. After I waited a few minutes, he walked out. He looked shocked when he saw me, and maybe a little embarrassed that I was showing up at his work. I stood up when I saw him, handing him the bouquet and thanking him for my flowers.

He explained that he thought it would've been too soon for him to call that day to set up another date, but that he wanted to at least acknowledge Valentine's Day. We agreed to talk later, and I headed back to work. I couldn't stop thinking about him and what a gentleman he was. We went out the next night, then the next night, and then every night after that.

I called my mom and told her about Roger almost immediately. She could hear in my voice how excited I was, and knew there was something special going on with him. All our plans for me to move back to France came to a grinding halt, but she never brought it up with me—she was just happy that I was happy.

Roger and I both felt the special connection between us, and talked for hours every time we got together and then more on the phone most nights too. We were both very honest with each other, sharing all about our past history and struggles. I think since we had both been married before, we knew how bad things could get with another person, and we knew what we wanted in a new relationship.

I found out what I thought was a wonderful, random coincidence at the time—that day I met Roger at the gym, he was only there because a friend of his invited him to come work out. He didn't normally go to that gym; he used one much closer to where he lived, which is why I never saw him there after the initial two times.

Most nights we would either go out to eat or he would cook for me at his well-kept townhouse. On the weekends, he took me out dancing since he knew how much I loved to dance. I met his two kids, who were twelve and sixteen at the time, that first week we were together. They were spending that school year with Roger, as he and his ex-wife lived several hours away from each other.

They were both very sweet to me, and we would all hang out together and have a great time. I had never imagined stepkids being a part of the picture for me, but I genuinely enjoyed spending time with Roger's kids. They were right at the age of my sisters back in France, so I felt like I was a big sister to them. They also gave me a unique window into another side of Roger's character, as I got to see what an amazing father he was to them. He could have let them live with his ex-wife, but he wanted them to be in his life as well.

About a week after we started seeing each other, he told me he loved me. We were just hanging out at his apartment, and he turned to look at me and said, "Hey, Karima…I love you." I remember it felt like my heart stopped in that moment as I looked into his eyes. I told him I loved him too, and I meant it. I had never met a man like him before, or felt this way about anyone else. He sent me the most beautiful emails, cards and notes, and truly made me feel so cared for and loved in a way I had never experienced.

Chapter 16

Rebirth

Yet to all who did receive him, to those who believed in his name, he gave the right to become children of God.
—John 1:12

Very early on, Roger told me that he was a new Christian and had just started going to church. I didn't really understand what that meant, but he knew that I was a non-practicing Muslim, and he invited me to come to his nondenominational church with him and his son and daughter. Of course I was willing to go with them, even though I didn't think it was for me.

Roger told me that he had grown up only going to church on the holidays, but when his kids moved in with him for a year just before he met me, he knew he needed to try to go more. He knew enough about church that he thought it would help him become a better man for his children, and ironically, Roger and his son both accepted Jesus as their Savior and got baptized together a few months before Roger met me.

A lot of different people had invited me to church over the years, but I always turned them down. People I knew back in Alabama and now in Savannah who went to clubs and partied every night went to church on Sundays, and would invite me. I always politely declined, thinking *How are you different from me? What is this church thing doing for you if we're still in the same club together every other day? Why would I want to go to someone's church when they are stuck doing all the same things as me?*

I had never really known anyone who was genuinely different because of their faith until I met Roger. I saw a difference in the way he treated me and others—he lived out kindness and love, and I was curious if his church and faith had something to do with that.

As we walked up to his church that first time, I was curious. When we got to the door, people immediately were greeting us like we were family. They were so kind and welcoming to me, a stranger. During the announcements, the speaker talked about the different projects in the community the church was involved in and different ways members could get involved. In my personal experience, Muslims didn't do anything like that for strangers in their community. I remember thinking *Okay, maybe these people are different. They love their God so much they are willing to go help random people for Him.*

I was already feeling at ease, but when the sermon started, I remember a strange feeling of peace washing over me. I went home that day thinking, *What was that? I've never felt like that before from being in a building with other people. These people are so nice and so loving.*

The pastor spoke about God as a friend, which intrigued me since I had never thought of Allah that way before. But the thing that got to me most was when he prayed: "Father God…" *Wait a second. God, our Father? So, not only do these people believe they can be close to God, but also that He is their Father?"* Allah was always described as lifted so high; he was in a position where no one could touch him. But this pastor was describing a God who sent His Son down to Earth to be with us and have a relationship with us and who *loved us?* I had to know more.

I had heard of Jesus when I was in Morocco, that he was a prophet sent to the Gentiles, and Muhammad was the prophet for the Arabs. But I didn't put it together that *Eissa*, the Jewish prophet, was the same Jesus worshiped by Christians until I came to the U.S. I had also seen pictures of the cross before, or people wearing cross jewelry, and never knew what it meant. There was something about it that had always attracted me, but I never bothered to learn what it symbolized.

As I continued going to church with Roger and his son and daughter, I learned who Jesus really was. He was God's Son, who gave up living in heaven to come down to Earth and live with humans. He lived a perfect, sinless life and died a tortured death at the hands of His own people, but rose from the dead three days later. The pastor explained that every person is a sinner, except for Jesus. But when He died, He took all our sin and paid the ultimate penalty we deserved. And, for anyone who believed in Him, His Spirit would come live inside that person, and they would be saved to one day go to heaven and be with God forever.

I could see the genuine love these people had for their God. I came to the realization that whatever they had was real, because it affected the way they acted. You could tell their faith was the driving force behind how they lived their lives. I could tell the same faith was behind how amazing Roger was and why he treated me so well. People would be praying at the altar at the end of services, and other people would just go up and pray with them. I had never seen an entire community be so kind and loving towards each other before. I was hungry for what they had, but unsure if I wanted to make the leap to a whole new religion.

Even though I wasn't actively practicing Islam and hadn't since I lived in Morocco, it was entrenched in me from such a young age that I was Muslim. That was who I was, what I was born to be, and it affected every facet of my life, from the way I ate, dressed and so on. I was never given a choice as a child as to what religion I wanted to follow—because I was Moroccan, I was Muslim. As I thought more about this new religion, I was honestly scared that if I became a Christian, Allah would strike me dead.

Fear held me back. I thought being Muslim was a part of my identity I was not supposed to change, and I was afraid that my family would disown me. When I would think about it, I felt ashamed, like I was letting my family down somehow.

My thoughts about Christianity weighed on my mind as the weeks passed. As adults who had both already been through previous marriages, Roger and I both knew very quickly that we wanted to get married, and we had many conversations about what our life would look like together. He assured me that he would never force me to choose any religion, and that he wanted to marry me regardless of my decisions in that area. He said he would love me no matter what, which, coming from my abusive background, was so important for me to hear. I was confident that his love for me wasn't dependent on my choices or his control over me.

However, when we asked his pastor if he would eventually marry us even though I was technically Muslim, he said he couldn't do that. Roger continued to assure me that he would marry me no matter what, that my religion was a personal decision that I had to make, and that we would just find someone else to marry us when the time came. I was grateful for him being willing to find someone else, but I felt bad that he would be going against his pastor's wishes.

I talked to my friend, Christina, at the salon about the whole situation, looking for advice. She was a Christian, but had never tried to force her religion on me. We had bonded because she was so friendly and kind, and over the course of the last year and a half I had been in Savannah, we had become close. She knew most of my backstory, and as I was explaining my dilemma to her, she started smiling and getting teary-eyed. I'll never forget what she said to me that day.

"Karima, it seems like God has been after you for a long time. I think it's time to surrender to Him."

Her words resonated in my heart and brought me such peace in that moment. I thought, *You know what, maybe this is what I've needed all along. I have nothing to lose—Islam hasn't ever done anything for me, and these Christians that I see are kind, loving people. Their lives are changed somehow. Maybe this will change my life too.*

I thought about every time I had encountered God over the past several years: the woman telling me, "God loves you" in Texas, hearing that sermon on TV when I was in my darkest season of life, getting the picture card of Jesus at Mr. Ji's shop, seeing pictures of the cross and being drawn to that image, meeting Roger and seeing how *real* his faith was…maybe God had been after my heart this whole time, and I hadn't seen it. Maybe this Father God could fill the hole in my life that I had ever since I could remember. Maybe He could fill my need for a relationship, for someone who would love me unconditionally.

Maybe this God was who I had been unknowingly, desperately searching for my whole life.

Once I made my decision, I remember going to Roger and telling him I wanted to be saved. He hugged me and was so happy for me. The very next day, April 12th, 2001, we called his pastor and told him I wanted to accept Christ and be baptized. I remember it was a weekday, so when Roger and I went into the church, it was only us, his son and daughter and the pastor.

His pastor got into the baptism pool with me, and helped me pray the sinner's prayer. Then he said, "I baptize you in the name of the Father, the Son and the Holy Spirit" and gently pushed me under the water. It was a surreal moment for all of us.

When I came up, I remember thinking, *Is that it? I'm a Christian now? I'm changed, just like that?* I didn't understand it all at that moment, but I knew something was different. I had accepted this Jesus into my heart, and was excited to be changed to be like the other Christians I had met at this church.

Roger's daughter was also baptized with me, so it was a doubly joyful day. We all went out to dinner that night to celebrate, and Roger bought me a Bible almost right away that I still have to this day. I couldn't wait to start my new life with Jesus and with Roger.

Chapter 17

Superman

This is my commandment, that you love one another as I have loved you. —John 15:12

About a month after we were dating, Roger started telling me to "be ready, because something big was gonna happen," or he'd say, "I'm planning something, and it's gonna be big!" I took that to mean he would be proposing soon, which of course I was thrilled about.

In some of our very first conversations, we put everything on the table. We were brutally honest with each other, because we didn't want there to be anything hidden. We knew that if we wanted to make this marriage work, we had to be completely transparent with each other, which served to strengthen our bond.

We had done a couple of planned activities and trips together with Roger's kids, like bowling or going to the beach, but I had only met his parents one time. I wanted to spend more time with them and get to know them better, but making the three-hour trip down to Nashville, Georgia from Savannah took up a whole day or two. We made plans to go again on April 15th, and we were supposed to leave right after I got off work—I had all my stuff packed in Roger's car.

I had nonstop, back-to-back appointments that day. Around

lunchtime, a long black limousine pulled up outside, and the driver walked in and asked, "Is Karima Baraka here?"

I was so busy and so confused as to why this guy would be asking for me. "Yeah, that's me," I said. He smiled and asked, "Can you come with me?" At this point, I knew this had to be Roger's doing, that maybe he wanted to treat me to a really nice trip. But I told the man I couldn't come because of how busy I was that day—I was literally in the middle of finishing a haircut when he walked in.

"Well, I have to take you somewhere," he said. I asked him to wait and quickly finished the haircut. Tammy, my boss, had heard the whole exchange, and I turned to her in my confusion: "I don't know what to do with this guy, but I know I can't leave. I have a book full of people scheduled to come in."

She laughed, and someone said, "You're good, those are all fake appointments!" Little did I know that Roger had called Tammy earlier that week, asking her to fill up my book with fake appointments so that I didn't take any real work that afternoon. She told me I needed to go, and proceeded to follow me into the limousine with some of my other coworkers.

Some of my other friends were already in the limo, along with a videographer holding a huge camera that was filming us. The song "Kryptonite" was playing on the speakers, and I started to realize that something was going on. I remember that I could feel my heart pumping through my body—*he's going to propose!*

We drove a couple of minutes down the road and pulled into a parking lot by the globe of Savannah, a local landmark built in the 1950s by the Savannah Gas Company to store natural gas. As I stepped out of the limo, I saw cameras and newspaper people standing outside around the 60-foot-tall globe, looking up. I followed their gaze and saw Superman! I had always been a big fan of Superman, ever since I was a teenager in France. He was dressed in the classic Superman costume, complete with the flowing red cape, standing in the classic Superman stance with his legs spread and hands on his hips. As I squinted up at the man, I realized—it was Roger!

I let out a squeal, and my jaw dropped. My first thought was, *Is he crazy?! He's gonna die, what is he doing up there?* He had a podium with a microphone set up for me, and his best friend led me to stand in front of it.

With Fox News filming, he greeted me from the top of the globe with a microphone; there was a whole sound system set up on the ground so I could hear him very well. He read a beautiful poem that he wrote, called "On the Top of the World," that went like this:

> *Truly, a lucky man am I to find a woman as wonderful as you. You make my days brighter, my nights more beautiful and you bring joy to everything I do.*
>
> *I never thought it possible to have a love that feels like this, and I must say, I am so amazed to find a love such as yours from a country so far away.*
>
> *I will start with your heart which is big enough for three. You bring kindness to everyone you greet and you're especially dear to me.*
>
> *Your beauty is stunning and your eyes make me never want to be away. Your touch, your kiss, your smile, your affection make me love you more every day.*
>
> *Your intelligence is intriguing and you are wise beyond*

your years. We can even finish each other's sentences, and we laugh ourselves into tears.

So here I am to ask for your hand, a special day for me. For I hope to finally have the love that will last an eternity.

Because of who you are and what you mean to me is why I feel so grand. You make me feel like I'm someone special like a King, a Prince and even Superman.

Say yes and I couldn't be more happy, and daily I'll thank the Lord, to have a person in my life who makes me feel like I'm on top of the world.

When he finished, he got down on one knee and asked the question my heart had been waiting for what felt like forever to hear:

"Karima, will you marry me?"

I was so nervous with all the people watching that I responded, "Yes, I do!" Everyone laughed, but I didn't care—I was going to marry my dream man. His best friend gave me the ring and a dozen roses while Roger climbed down. He gave me the biggest hug once he was on the ground. I couldn't believe what was happening; it felt like I was in a fairytale.

I found out later how much preparation he had to do to make his grand proposal idea happen, from signing a waiver to climb up the globe (yes, he wore a harness!), to contacting the news and getting them to come, to renting the limo and getting all our friends involved to be there and help.

We took a few pictures there together, and then left for a surprise weekend trip to Amelia Island, where he had planned several fun activities for us to do together. We even rode horses on the beach, which was something I had talked about always wanting to do. His thoughtfulness and kindness towards me continued to blow me away—I couldn't believe I was getting to marry this incredible man who loved me so much.

We both wanted a big wedding with friends and family, but since my family lived so far away we decided to wait a year so they could plan to attend. So, on April 18th, 2001, we were officially married at Roger's church by his pastor, just six days after I was baptized there. It was a very intimate ceremony with just Roger, me and his pastor. We didn't want to wait to start our life together, and I trusted that we would be able to plan the bigger wedding the following year.

After the ceremony, I moved into Roger's two-bedroom townhouse with him and his kids, but we started working on building a little three-bedroom prefab house for our new family almost right away. We knew we wanted kids eventually, so more space was going to be a necessity. My move was easy, since I was still renting a room from a friend and didn't have to get out of a lease.

Right after we got married, we sat down together and talked over what we were going to do to make this marriage different from what we had both experienced before. We threw out all of our old love letters, pictures and mementos with other people, deciding then and there that our marriage was going to be completely united. Even though we were still very young in our faith, we knew we had Christ in us, so we prayed that He would protect our marriage.

Something that weighed heavy on my heart during this conversation was the abuse that I had gone through. After my divorce, I realized how I had truly escaped an abusive relationship, although I hadn't seen it that way at the time. I remember telling Roger, "You know my past. I will treat you like a king, and serve you hand and foot and be with you until the day I die. I'll never leave you. But if there is any unfaithfulness or any kind of abuse, mental or physical, it doesn't matter how many kids we have—I'm walking out and I won't look back. I will not go through that again, and I will not allow another man to treat me like that again."

We talked about what the Bible said about wives and husbands and how they were supposed to treat each other, and we agreed to try our best to meet those standards every day. We also agreed to get help if we had any issues that started to come up—neither of us wanted to run at the first sign of trouble. However, with my past, it was really important to me that I was clear on how I felt about abuse and what I had gone through.

After that, we went out and tattooed our left ring fingers with each others' names, wanting to make a physical mark of the permanence of our relationship. It's the only tattoo on my body to this day. We committed to work on our marriage and love each other well, so we wouldn't lose this special thing that we had. It was almost like we put a bubble around ourselves.

As we started our life together, I caught myself wondering every once in a while *Okay, what is wrong with this guy? He has to have something wrong with him.* After my past experience, a small part of me was worried that he would change once we said our vows. But I trusted him, trusted his faith and his love, and knew that I loved him in a totally different way than I had loved anyone else before. I felt safe with him, something I had never felt with a guy before. I knew I had snagged a trophy husband, and I felt like a million dollars any time I was with him. Our time together only got sweeter, and he continued to treat me the way he always had.

I was so, so happy. I truly couldn't believe it—I was *finally* living my dream. I was married to a handsome, kind American man who treated me like a princess. He was smart, romantic, honest and trustworthy. His quiet, steadfast love anchored me. Somehow, even after all I'd been through, I had so much faith in the man that he was and knew I had made the right decision in marrying him.

We continued going to church together every Sunday, but that was really the depth of our involvement in Christianity at the time. We brought our Bibles, listened to the sermon and came back home. The church was almost an hour away from us, which made it difficult to get involved in any of the other events going on. Since my faith had never changed the way I acted as an adult before, I didn't know how this new faith was going to change me.

I thought I would magically become a different person, which I soon realized was not going to happen. I didn't tell my mom or the rest of my family about my decision until several years later, because I was afraid of their reactions and I didn't know how to fully explain my decision. We still didn't have Skype or social media back in 2001, so I was still only calling my family in France once a week for a few minutes at a time with a calling card. I didn't want to "waste" the little time I had arguing with my mom about my religion. I knew they wouldn't be thrilled. I was especially terrified of my grandmother and what she would think, so I kept my new faith to myself.

That summer of 2001, we took our first international trip together and visited Morocco for about three weeks. My mom and sisters came down from France, so Roger was able to meet almost everyone all at the same time. My stepdad unfortunately had to work, so he couldn't make it that year.

I had tried to prepare Roger for all the different traditions and customs of Morocco, but didn't think to mention the traditional Moroccan greeting when you visit someone's home. I don't know why, but the host greets their guests with milk and dates for them to enjoy. When we arrived at my grandmother's house that summer, my family hadn't seen me in several years and met us at the door with this treat.

Roger had never had a date before, but wanting to be polite, he took one right away and popped the whole thing into his mouth, not realizing it had a pit. My family was so excited to meet him, so they were all talking to him, but all he could do was nod and smile and try to chew the date. He told me later that the whole time it was in his mouth he was about to barf. Somehow, he managed to get the seed out on the side of his mouth and drink milk to wash the rest of the date down. We had a good laugh later about the whole experience.

My family loved Roger. He connected instantly with them, and made an intentional effort to spend time with them and get to know them. I think they could all see how much he loved and cared for me, a stark contrast from the last guy I had brought to meet them.

The person who loved Roger the most out of everyone, though—my grandmother! She absolutely adored him. She would serve him herself, or make other people bring him anything that she thought he needed. I remember one of my uncles telling me, "This is a really great guy," which meant so much to me.

One night, we were playing Moroccan music and belly dancing together, and my grandmother actually got up and danced with me. I hold that memory near and dear to my heart to this day—it was such a special moment for me. The distance of time and space helped me see how my grandmother really did love her family; she just didn't know how to show it. I could see that all her children were still seeking acceptance from her the same way I was, and even after the way she had treated all of us, we were still starving for her attention.

Despite her happiness in having us visit, she was still the same person I had grown up with. One day, I came downstairs for the day wearing a blouse and pants, and as soon as she saw me she said, "You're not wearing that. Go change." Of course, not wanting to cause problems, I went back and changed into a dress.

Surprisingly, I got a lot of her attention that trip. She decided that while we were there, she was going to throw us a Moroccan wedding. She organized everything, from inviting all the family and friends, making food and decorating the whole house. She did *henna* on my hands and feet and gave me a beautiful blue and gray silk *takashita* to wear, which I still have.

We bought Roger a traditional Moroccan groom outfit as well, and I even went to a hair salon and had my hair and makeup done for the day. I loved every detail, but the best part was that my grandmother was doing all this to celebrate *me*, and made me the center of attention. I felt so special and a little overwhelmed at her kindness. It was an all-day event, with music and all different instruments playing all day. We ate and danced and had a great time, and it is a memory with my family that I will cherish forever.

Another really interesting thing that happened on that trip was that I was able to meet my biological dad's family for the first time. It was my mom's idea—she knew where they lived and had stayed in touch with them here and there over the years. One day of our trip, she and my two sisters took the train with Roger and I from Marrakech to Casablanca, and then we took a taxi from there to Mohammadia. We went to my grandparents' house, where they had gathered that whole side of the family to meet me.

It was a little awkward at first, meeting my grandma, grandpa, aunts and uncles, knowing that we were close relatives but not having any type of connection with them. But they were all so kind, and they told me stories about my dad. They even gave me a picture of him, which was cool since I had only seen one picture of him, which was my mom's of him and me together. He was a very handsome man, tall with fair skin, brown eyes and thick brown hair.

They also told me that after he and my mom got divorced, he remarried and had a son, my stepbrother, who later came to meet us in Marrakech. We all chatted for several hours and had a very nice visit; they asked questions about me and I was able to ask questions about them and my dad. They had a feast for us there that evening, and we spent the night and left the next morning.

Roger and I had a near disaster that night. We snuck away for a moment to the third floor of the house, which had an open outside area, to smoke a quick cigarette. When we finished, we were trying to figure out what to do with the cigarette butts. We didn't want to leave them, but we also didn't want to carry them back downstairs.

Roger saw an open pipe, and quickly threw his down, thinking it led to the street outside the house. I did the same thing, but then suddenly it dawned on us that the pipe was probably attached to the kitchen, since they had a big stove. Terrified, we rushed downstairs into the kitchen, and sure enough the pipe hole was right next to the stove, and the cigarette butts were sitting right there on the countertop, inches away from the food. Thankfully, we were able to dispose of them before anyone noticed, and they didn't make it into the dinner pot!

When we left the next morning, we hugged everyone goodbye and headed out into the city. One of my dad's brother's took us on a little tour of the city before we left. We couldn't find a train to take us back, so we rode the three hours back home to Marrakech squished into the back of a taxi. The driver drove his taxi like a race car, which made it a terrifying trip as he weaved in and out of traffic the whole way back.

It was interesting when we got back to my grandmother's house, because somehow she found out where we had gone and was furious. I remember her screaming at me, saying, "Why would you go over there? They didn't want you in the first place—they were going to throw you in the ocean!" I think she was just very protective over her own and didn't know how to express it. My mom stepped in right away, and started to really get into it with my grandmother. Thankfully, my grandmother stopped yelling quickly after that; I think she remembered their fight from long ago in 1986 when I left, and she didn't want history to repeat itself.

Probably my favorite memory from that trip was when I walked Roger out to the souk where I used to beg for money as a little girl. Standing there with him was a surreal moment for me. I don't think I realized how truly blessed I was until that moment, standing in the arms of my American man in the exact place where I used to dream about him. I remember feeling so grateful to God for blessing me with all that He had given.

Chapter 18

Growing Roots

But now, this is what the LORD says— he who created you, Jacob, he who formed you, Israel: "Do not fear, for I have redeemed you; I have summoned you by name; you are mine." —Isaiah 43:1

We flew back to the U.S. in late August of 2001, landing in JFK airport before our connection to Savannah. However, the flight was delayed a whole day, so Roger and I made the most of it and went to a nice Japanese restaurant for dinner before spending the night at a hotel in Manhattan.

It was my first time in New York City, so I was in awe at the buildings and the billboards—I didn't mind our little detour at all. In the taxi on our way back to the airport the next day, Roger tried to point out all the different landmarks that we could see. I remember staring out the window enamored by the cityscape, when he pointed and said, "Look! Those are the twin towers!" He told me we would have to come back another time and spend more time in the city, which I was excited about.

Two weeks later, we were both back to our regular lives and work. It was a normal Tuesday, and I was in the middle of a haircut when I heard, "Oh my God!" from the back of the shop. My boss was in the back room coloring a patient's hair, which was also where our only small TV was located. She said a plane had just hit one of the twin towers.

Our shop was within walking distance of the military base, so we had a lot of military guys in the shop, and we all started talking, wondering what had just happened. Of course it was tragic, but we all assumed it must have been some type of accident. But then, just fifteen minutes later, the second plane hit, and everyone started freaking out. I started hearing the words "terrorists" and "attack," which was so frightening.

Roger called almost immediately after the second plane hit, wanting to make sure I was okay. The whole day was eerie—it seemed surreal, what we were watching unfold on the TV right before our eyes. Everyone was scared; we didn't know how many planes were coming, or where they were going to crash next.

When the news began broadcasting that the attack had been by an Islamic extremist group, Roger was very worried about me. He warned me to be careful in case anyone tried to harass me as an Arabic woman. Thankfully, most people who assumed my ethnicity thought I was Hispanic, and I didn't have the Arabic accent since I had lived in France before moving to the U.S. I never had anyone approach or harass me in connection with my ethnicity, but it was definitely something I was worried about.

Throughout that whole experience, Roger and I sensed God's provision. If our trip dates had been a little different, we could have easily been in the city in danger at the time of the attacks. The fact that we had seen the towers just two weeks before made the whole thing more frightening, and made us so grateful for God's protection.

Learning that the attackers were Muslim also shook me spiritually. I remember thinking, *What kind of religion is this? How can this be a religion of peace, if there are people out there killing other people in the name of Allah?* I realize that many religions have different extremist groups attached to them, but this was my first experience seeing Muslims behave this way. I didn't even know radical Muslims existed, since my family wasn't like that at all. I was still working through separating my identity and religion from my ethnicity at the time, and watching this situation unfold in front of me made me think more deeply about what I believed.

At the beginning of the fall of 2001, our first house in Pooler, Georgia was completed, and we moved in. It was the first time either of us had lived in a house, which made it extra special. His children went back to live with their mom that summer before, so when we moved in, it was just the two of us living there. His son came back to live with us for that school year.

Right before we were supposed to make our first payment, we faced our first big challenge as a married couple. Roger came home from work one day with tears in his eyes and a box in hand—he had been let go from his job. The company was struggling and had to make several personnel cuts, and he was one of the ones let go. When he came in like that and said, "Honey, I lost my job," my heart almost tore in two—it was so hard seeing him like that. I hugged him and told him it was going to be okay, and that we would figure it out.

To be honest, I wasn't worried. I wasn't dependent on God at the time—I was still learning about Him and still didn't totally understand what faith in Him looked like. However, I had full faith in Roger. He was so responsible and smart. Right after we got married he had sat down with me and gone over our finances, making a budget and talking everything over with me.

I completely trusted him, and I was so content just being with him; we could have lived in a cardboard box for all I cared. All that mattered to me was that we had each other.

He found a new job at a different trucking company a few weeks later, and then the following summer of 2002, we finally had our bigger wedding. Using all the bridal magazines I could get my hands on, I planned the whole thing myself. Our venue was a beautiful golf course on the marsh, and we had a DJ, caterer, photographer—it was the real deal.

My trust in Roger had grown as he continued to deliver on his promises as a loving, faithful husband. I was overjoyed walking down the aisle in my white dress, seeing him at the other end. About fifty people attended, including close friends and my family who came from France, which made the day even more special. I was nervous, sweaty and shaky just like any other bride, but beyond thrilled to marry the man of my dreams (again!) and have the wedding I had fantasized about for so long. We even went on a short honeymoon afterwards at the beach on Tybee Island.

* * *

Later that year, Roger realized he wasn't happy at his new job. He had worked there for about a year, but one night, he told me he had thought about starting his own trucking business for a long time. I encouraged him, because I knew he could succeed at anything. I remember him asking, "What if it doesn't work out? What if we lose everything?" He was so concerned with taking care of me and our family, which I loved. But I also wanted him to pursue his dream. "We'll still be okay," I said.

"We have God and we have each other. I believe in you, and I think you will be great at whatever you decide to do."

At the time, we didn't have much extra money, so he reached out to the owner of his old company that had let him go and asked if he could use an old trailer that was parked by the building as his new office. He also asked if the company had any extra computers lying around anywhere. His old boss gave him the green light to use the space, and told him there were some old computers in a storage shed he was welcome to use. Roger found pieces of different working computers in there and basically built his own computer out of the parts and started working in his little makeshift office. Once he got everything set up, he quit his other job so he could fully focus on his new business.

He worked so hard, doing many late nights and weekends trying to get it off the ground. Eventually, he was able to move into an actual office space and hire some staff. Within a year, he had made enough to buy a five-acre plot of land, put a double wide trailer on it and hire even more people.

That fall of 2002 back when he first started his business, we made another change that ended up dramatically impacting our future as well. Because our little home was almost an hour away from our church, we wanted to try to find something a little closer. We loved the pastor and the people there, but it was just too far away for us to really get involved in anything they had going on, and we both were feeling a pull to get more involved in church. I realized I wasn't "changing into a new person," and thought maybe I needed to be in church a little more.

Our pastor there who married us also passed away from cancer soon after we made the decision to look for a new church. When we walked into his viewing at the church, his wife was standing at the door, greeting people with a smile. I remember thinking, *How is she standing there smiling when her husband just passed away? How is she able to hold herself together?*

That stayed with me for a long time, since I thought about how I didn't think I could be like that if Roger were to ever pass away. Many years later, I realized it was her relationship with God that was sustaining her and her belief that she would see her husband again one day in their heavenly home. But I didn't have that level of hope and trust in my life yet.

One of Roger's friends knew we were looking for a church, and invited us to try his. So, one Sunday, we drove twenty minutes from our house in Pooler to a non-denominational church in Effingham County, Georgia. After one visit, we knew this was the church for us. We loved the pastor, and everyone there was so welcoming and kind.

As we continued attending over the next few months, we began talking about moving closer. Roger's business was also in the same area, and the school districts were great too. My stepson had come back to live with us for that school year and we were considering having kids soon, so knowing there were good schools in that area was a huge positive.

2003 was a big year for us—we visited my family in France that summer, and I was filled with pride for my mom; at the encouragement of my sisters and stepdad, she had learned to drive and even had a driver's license. She was also taking French classes to improve her reading and writing, and I had a fresh appreciation for her intelligence and determination.

When we returned from the trip, we put our house in Pooler on the market to see what would happen. Within two months, the house ended up selling for $20,000 more than what we had paid to build it. We could see God orchestrating everything to make this move happen, and we had a lot of peace that it was the right decision for our family.

We moved into an apartment in Effingham County, and started the process of building a house there in late 2003. We decided this house was going to be our dream house and that we wanted to put down roots in this area, so the planning was much more in depth than our last house build. We had a great time designing the architecture together and making the house a blend of both our backgrounds and personalities. The entire project took just over a year to finish.

At the same time our house was being built, another longtime dream came true—I started my very own hair salon. In the same way that I was supportive of Roger and his dreams, he was supportive of mine. We rented a building in Effingham County, remodeled it together and purchased everything I needed, from furniture and tanning beds to color perms and hair stations. I talked to Tammy about the whole thing beforehand, and she had a lot of helpful tips for me to get started; we are still friends to this day.

Once we had everything set up, I hired a few employees and my salon, called French Connection, was up and running. My first employee was a girl right out of cosmetology school, Jenny. It was so rewarding to get to teach her everything I knew and be her mentor. Now she owns her own shop! I also learned how stressful yet rewarding it could be to run my own business. I loved my little shop and customers, but it kept me busy, working hard to make it a success.

Another milestone that year was when Roger and I quit smoking. As we planned to try to have our own kids soon, we knew it was an unhealthy habit we needed to get rid of. It was very difficult to do, but doing it together with a purpose in mind helped us a lot. I tried off and on for a while before finally kicking the habit towards the end of that year. The patches helped me a lot, and I even used lollipops for a while just to have something in my hand. Roger used jawbreakers, which was funny when he would order a whole box of them. Even though we both had our different ways of overcoming the habit, working through that together was something that brought us closer.

By Christmas 2004, our beautiful new house was finally finished. Knowing how important my family is to me, Roger has always made them a priority too, with them either coming here or us going to them at least once a year. My parents and sisters made the trip to the U.S. to celebrate with us that year, and it was extra special since we were able to celebrate Christmas in our new house all together.

That was the first time they were exposed to my new faith. I was still afraid to tell my mom that I was a Christian, but we were going to church regularly, and I didn't want to skip going just because they were visiting. We asked them if they would come with us, and they said yes, so they watched us sing on the praise team and listened to the whole sermon. They didn't seem to think much of it at the time; it was just something we did that they didn't understand.

Chapter 19

Surrender

Being confident of this, that he who began a good work in you will carry it on to completion until the day of Christ Jesus. —Philippians 1:6

When I first got saved, I didn't fully understand what it meant—I just knew I believed in Jesus and His sacrifice on the cross for me. I thought my life would start to change to become "better" all by itself. Little did I know how God was going to get a hold of my heart.

Soon after I was saved and baptized, I was sitting in church with Roger and heard a sermon from our pastor about drinking. Still learning as a new believer, I remember thinking, *Wait a minute. No drinking? No smoking? No going to clubs? What am I going to do? Those are all things that I do pretty regularly—what have I gotten myself into?*

Both mine and Roger's faith was pretty shallow for a while, with the extent of our religious action being going to church on Sunday mornings. But Roger and I were slowly learning more and more about Christianity. I didn't know that a lot of the things I had been doing and the way that I had been living were wrong at all, so it took a while for me to realize that, accept it and want to change. It was a process of giving up control of things in my lifestyle that were not honoring God.

The first thing that started to change was the way I dressed. After my divorce, I dressed however I wanted as an expression of my freedom, since that was an area I was controlled in before. Most of my clothes were revealing, which I didn't think twice about at the time.

Roger was so patient and kind with me as I worked through the different areas of my life that needed to change. About six months into our marriage, he commented on the way I dressed for the first time. "Honey, you really don't need to dress like that. I'm not going to tell you what to do, but I'm just saying, you don't have to. You're so beautiful, and dressing like that… you attract the wrong attention."

When he said that, my first thought was, *Oh boy. Here we go—Mr. Control. There is no way I'm listening to this. He's not going to tell me what to do! I'm fine.* After what I had been through, I wasn't about to give up anything I felt was my right. This issue was our first disagreement as a husband and wife, and we had many conversations about it. He felt disrespected by my disregard of his opinion and protective of me as he saw other men staring at me out in public.

But he was so gentle with me, and not forceful at all with his words when we talked about it. It took me a while to grow out of my defensive reactions towards him and realize that what he was saying was coming from a place of love and care for me, not a desire to control.

At one point, a lady from our church got up the courage to say something to me too. I also cut her hair, so we had chatted a few times before she mentioned that the way I dressed in church was not appropriate. I blew her off, but her words stuck with me and I started to realize that maybe something really was wrong with how I was dressing. *Maybe Roger is right*, I remember thinking.

In the beginning, I was innocent and unaware that many of my habits were not the best choices, but the longer I was a Christian, the more I started to feel icky about them. Conviction started to take hold of me as I watched other Christians and noticed how their actions made them different.

But the key for me was *how* to change. For example, I didn't know what it meant to dress modestly—did I have to wear a sack to be modest? Of course not, but I didn't know. It took a long time for me to figure out what kind of clothes to look for. Something practical that helped me years down the road was when I found a pamphlet on modesty in the bathroom of a church I was visiting. It talked about how to check yourself before leaving the house, wearing a tank top under revealing or see-through tops and wearing shorts under shorter dresses. These were practical pieces of advice for me to learn a new way of presenting myself to the world. As I changed this particular aspect of my life, I realized that I was getting more comments on my beauty, not fewer. More importantly, people approached me more respectfully and treated me more as an equal.

A big help in my spiritual journey and this battle with dressing modestly was when we started to get more involved in our new church in 2003. We began volunteering in the nursery and on the praise team, and the more we got plugged into the Christian community, the more people were pouring Christ into us. Eventually, we started teaching Awana, the kids' Sunday school, together, which was a huge learning experience for us both. Not growing up in Christian homes, we both heard many of the "classic" Bible stories for the first time this way, as we would have to prepare our lessons and learn what we were about to teach the kids in our class.

Serving together not only helped us grow in our spiritual lives, but also in our marriage relationship. As we grew in Christ individually, we grew together. I didn't start reading my Bible regularly right away—it was a process for me as I slowly learned more about this God I had chosen to follow. The more I learned, the more I wanted to learn and grow.

As the months passed, Roger and I both started to realize the importance of a personal relationship with Jesus. It wasn't only about going to church on Sundays and reading our Bibles—we could see the changes in our lives happening the more we learned and were a part of a loving church community.

But, even with all the wonderful things in my life that were happening, I still quietly struggled with one certain aspect of my new faith—surrender. My friend's words from before I got saved replayed in my mind often: "Karima, it seems like God has been after you for a long time. I think it's time to surrender to Him." The more I learned about my new faith, the more I realized I wasn't fully surrendered. I hadn't given up my whole self to God. Deep in my heart, I wasn't sure if I wanted to.

I remember thinking at one point, *Yeah, okay, I'm gonna surrender. Dream on.* With my history of abuse, that word left a bitter taste in my mouth. My whole life, from growing up Muslim to being in an abusive marriage, it was reinforced to me that I wasn't as good as men; that I was worth less. The word surrender felt like I was leaving myself wide open to be taken advantage of, to be trapped, to be hurt. And I was not going to let that happen again. Could I really trust God enough to give Him all of me?

In January of 2004, Roger and I attended a couples' conference with our new church. This thought of surrender had been weighing on my mind, especially in light of the whole modesty issue that Roger and I had been working through. I desperately didn't want to give up what I felt like was my independence and autonomy to my husband or to God—it felt too dangerous.

For one of the sessions during the conference, the husbands and wives were split into two different groups. In our women's group, the speaker used a book called *Every Woman's Battle* to share with us, and it was all about surrender in the specific areas where I was struggling. She talked about women surrendering to their husbands as the leader of their home, and how God had created men and women equal but different in a good and beautiful way. She talked about how we honor the Lord in the way we dress and act. She explained that this choice wasn't ultimately for our husbands, it was for the Lord.

As this woman spoke, it felt like her words directly pierced my heart. The Lord orchestrated this moment specifically for me, to hear exactly what I needed to hear, from a woman's perspective. At that moment, I realized Roger said what he did about how I dressed because he loved me. *He's not trying to control me, he's trying to protect me. He truly loves and cares about me and wants others to see me in a good light.* This realization made me love him more, and I knew that what he said was right.

Even more than that, I realized how Roger's love for me paralleled God's love for me. God wasn't trying to control me—He wanted what was best for me too, and He wanted to use me as an example of His love to others. My trust in my husband and my trust in the Lord grew together as I saw their faithful characters revealed, and that's when I was truly motivated to change my life. I found a new desire in my heart to do whatever

God asked me to do, which in turn helped me to trust Roger more and lean on his guidance and wisdom.

Roger made me fall in love even more with God, and God made me fall in love even more with Roger. During that session, it felt like a veil had been lifted from my eyes, and the amazing gift of my life with Roger became sweeter in a whole new way.

For the last session of the conference, the speaker had vases that were broken into pieces at the front of the room. He explained how every person had brokenness in their lives, but that God could heal and restore. He talked about the importance of forgiveness, and how crucial it was to give all our hurts to God. At the end of his talk, he extended an invitation: "If you need to forgive someone, or ask for forgiveness yourself, come and pick up a broken piece of pottery. Make things right with God, ask Him to make you whole in Him and then leave that broken piece at the altar."

My feet moved before my brain knew what was happening—the Holy Spirit did a work in my heart that day. As I knelt down at the altar, clutching that broken piece of a vase in my fingers, tears streamed down my face. I laid it all at Jesus' feet that day—my grandmother's abuse, everything my ex-husband had done, my abortion—all of it. I forgave everyone who had ever hurt me that day, and received forgiveness myself for all the things I had done.

The peace I felt was indescribable, and I heard God whisper in my heart: *You don't have to worry about these things any more, my daughter. You have found me, and I am Your Father. I love you, and I will never leave you or forsake you. I forgive you for everything you've done—that is why my Son died on the cross for you. Leave everything at my feet.*

I didn't realize what a heavy burden all the pain and hurt I had been carrying was until I let it go. I knelt at the foot of the cross that day and truly surrendered my life to Jesus. I physically felt like I had just put down a heavy pack, and I felt so light and free.

Before that day, I had many nightmares about my grandmother and ex-husband. I couldn't think about them without feeling angry and bitter. But after that night, I never had another nightmare about them again. I could actually have compassion for them and pray for them, that God would save them too.

I had also been haunted by guilt about my abortion, especially once I learned that it was wrong. I heard about it in a sermon soon after my salvation, and thought, *Oh my gosh. My baby was alive, and I got rid of it.* My heart was so heavy every time I thought about it. I had struggled for years thinking about that precious life; how old he or she would have been, and what they would have been like. I told myself I should have fought for that baby harder than I did, or at least given it up for adoption.

But God, in His great love and mercy, took all that guilt from me that night. I left all that shame on the altar, and God forgave me. I now rejoice knowing that my child is in heaven with Him, and I so look forward to the day when I get to meet them.

To this day when I pray and call God my Father, I truly believe that He is. Growing up without an earthly father makes my relationship with Him even more precious. He is the only one who has never betrayed me or let me down—He is always there. I thank Him every day for what He has done in my life.

That conference was a huge milestone in my spiritual life. Again, nothing magically changed afterward; the changes in my life were still a process of getting rid of old habits and creating new ones. That process is still going on today! But I learned that knowing about Jesus and having a relationship with Him are two very different things.

Having a relationship with Him changes everything, from the way you think to the way you treat others, to the way you see Jesus. He has done everything for me. He is everything. All my growth in Him is based on that.

Roger has been an encouragement in that growth too. It's been such a gift to get to grow in our faith together. Before I read my Bible daily, he had made that a habit in his life. I'd see him reading it every day, first thing in the morning. His consistency spurred me to do that for myself. He taught me the importance of spending time in God's Word above all else. The more I read it, the more I trust God and have peace in my daily life. It's like my morning coffee—I need it every day.

Chapter 20

Growing a Family, Growing in Faith

*Children are a heritage from the L*ORD*, offspring a reward from him.* —Psalm 127:3

In the summer of 2005, we went to Morocco again together, this time taking Roger's son with us. We had a great time together seeing all my family, and that trip prompted us to start considering having our own kids sooner rather than later. We had talked about making sure we had a few years of marriage under our belts before we started trying, but now that we were settled in our new house and both working our own successful businesses, it seemed like the perfect time. I planned to take off work for a few months after having a baby, but I definitely wanted to go back to work after that. I had worked so hard to build a successful business, and I enjoyed my independence in that area.

To celebrate our decision to start a family, Roger and I went on a short "baby-making" cruise to the Bahamas in October that year. One of the few nights we were on the ship, we went to a little bar to hang out and listen to music. They were having a karaoke night, and even though Roger is an introverted guy, he loves to sing and loves karaoke. He has a great voice, and even used to be the lead singer in a rock band when he was younger. So, he went up to the microphone to sing, but before he started he introduced himself by saying, "Good evening everyone! Before I sing this song, I just wanted to let you all know that my wife and I are here to make a baby! This is our baby cruise!"

I was sitting at our table so embarrassed as he gestured to me as his wife and people started chuckling and applauding. I was like, *Are you kidding me?! You had to say that to everybody?!* After that night, it seemed like everyone on board would come up to us smiling and ask, "so, how's it going?" I was embarrassed, but Roger thought it was hilarious.

We were very blessed that I was able to get pregnant quickly. When the test read positive two days before Thanksgiving, I almost couldn't believe it. I was at work and randomly decided to take a test to see if maybe I was pregnant. I had taken a few before with Roger already, but they had all been negative. We were having Thanksgiving dinner with Roger's family, so I decided to keep it a secret from Roger and surprise them all at the same time with the good news. Bad idea.

Thanksgiving evening, I took another test so I could show them the proof, and then came downstairs to the kitchen where the whole family was together before dinner. I handed it to Roger, who didn't know what was going on for a second. He asked, "What is that?" and then realized, "Oh my gosh—you're pregnant!" I told him I had known for a couple of days, and he was a little disappointed. "Seriously?" he said. "You should have told me!" I said I was sorry, and the joy of my news overshadowed any other feelings after that. Everyone was so thrilled to be welcoming a new little member of the family.

My whole family was so excited too—I was the first granddaughter, having the first great-grandchild. My parents had always wanted a boy since they had three girls, but my stepdad had always said, "Don't worry about it, Karima will give us a boy." So when we went to the sonogram appointment where we found out the baby was a boy, I couldn't wait to tell them.

Unfortunately, I was pretty sick and nauseous my whole pregnancy. I was still able to work, but it became more difficult the bigger I got. I'm normally a petite 5'3", so as I got into the last trimester I was all belly. But I loved the whole pregnancy process and it was all very special, from my belly growing, to seeing him at the appointments and hearing his heartbeat, to feeling his kicks inside me. I read so many books on how to be a mom and take care of my baby, I could've written my own book, and I baby-proofed our whole house from top to bottom. I was so excited to meet him.

By the spring of 2006, I had lived in the U.S. for just over thirteen years. The thought of becoming an American citizen had crossed my mind before, but now being six months pregnant I started thinking about it more seriously. I realized that I wanted to have access to the same things my son would have access to, being born as an American citizen. I never wanted to be afraid that something crazy would happen with my green card and I would have to be separated from my husband and child.

So, I learned what I had to do to pass the citizenship test and started studying. I learned so much about the American government, from who our senators were to the different amendments to the Constitution. The test had one hundred questions, so I had to be prepared for anything. Once I was ready, we went to Atlanta and I passed the test on the first try. It was a surreal moment when the worker there gave me my naturalization paperwork. I, Karima Burdette, was a citizen of the United States of America! I remember thinking, *Oh my gosh. I can't believe I'm an American. Who would've thought!* It was and still is one of the greatest privileges of my life.

I worked all the way up until two weeks before our baby was born. My mom and sisters came at that point and stayed for six weeks to help me, which was such a blessing. On July 30th at 2 a.m., I woke up to some painful cramps. Roger and I and my mom and sisters drove straight to the hospital in Savannah, but when we arrived I was still only one centimeter dilated and the doctor wanted to send me home.

I begged them to keep me since we lived over forty minutes away and I was in a decent amount of pain. They agreed, but I couldn't eat anything since there was the chance I'd have to have surgery if something went wrong. I chewed on ice chips and labored all day for 22 hours—it was the most exhausting day of my life. By late that night, I was still only seven centimeters dilated, the baby was stuck and his heartbeat was starting to get a little irregular. The doctors told me I needed a c-section. At that point, I just wanted the baby out.

I got an epidural and then was taken to surgery—it was all over so quickly. It felt like minutes and then Roger was handing me our beautiful baby boy. It was an incredible moment, holding him for the first time. I forgot all the pain as I looked into his eyes, and felt more love for our little baby than I even thought possible. We named him Zecharia, after the Biblical prophet, and called him Zech for short.

He was a healthy, beautiful baby, weighing almost eight pounds. My sisters saw him in the nursery while I was getting sewn up after surgery and said he opened his big brown eyes and looked straight at them.

Once we were home, I'd wake up in the mornings and just stare at him. *I had a baby? Is this life even real?* I felt immeasurably blessed. After a few months with him, I realized that I couldn't leave him to go back to work. If my mom or Roger's family lived closer, I probably would've left him with them, but the closest family to us was four hours away. We were also still relatively new to the area, and I didn't feel comfortable leaving him with a babysitter.

When I talked to Roger about me staying home with Zech, he was so supportive and encouraging. I felt bad for my customers that I wouldn't be going back; I had some who would drive an hour to see me. But the more I thought about staying home, the more peace I had, and I knew it was the right decision for our family. I was able to continue managing my shop while I was home with Zech, so at least I didn't have to fully step out of what I had worked so hard to build.

God always works through difficult or painful situations to accomplish His purpose, and my recovery from my c-section was no different. An area of my spiritual life where I struggled greatly for many years was sharing the gospel. I knew at this point that I should be telling others about the wonderful gift Jesus was to me, but I was so afraid of how they would react, especially my family. My weeks of recovery unexpectedly turned into an opportunity one Sunday morning a month or two after Zech was born as I made my weekly call to my family in France.

Sometimes, we talked during the week, but even to this day we always connect on Sunday afternoons. That specific Sunday, I Skyped my mom and stepdad and was telling them that I had just gotten home from church. My mom quickly responded, saying, "Aren't you still recovering? Why did you go to church?

You don't need to be going there, it's not doing anything for you."

While she was talking, I felt the Holy Spirit moving in my heart. *This is a chance to tell her about the truth that you know. You need to share it with her.* I took a deep breath and prayed, *Speak through me, Father.* My heart felt like it was thumping out of my chest.

"Mom, I'm a Christian. I follow Jesus now, and I want to go to church every week so that I can learn more about Him."

Immediately, she replied, "Uh, no. What do you mean you're a Christian? No, you're not becoming a Christian. You're Muslim. You're Moroccan. You can't become a Christian, you're Moroccan."

"Mom, being Moroccan and being a Christian are two different things," I explained. "I will always be Moroccan, because it's my origin, where I was born. But Christianity is a religion, and I can change my religion if this is what I believe to be true."

She listened but still didn't agree. "No, you're Moroccan, you're Muslim, that's it."

This was exactly the situation I was terrified of when I chose to become a Christian five years earlier. I didn't know what to say then, but now, I knew where I could find my identity, and it wasn't in my ethnicity.

"Mom, listen. I love you, and I love my family, and I'll always be Moroccan. I did not kill anyone and I'm not disrespecting you, and that's how you're making me feel, like I've disowned you in some way or like I've done something horrible. But I haven't. I found a God who loves me for who I am, not because of the things that I do. He truly loves me and wants a relationship with me. I believe He has saved me from my sins. I believe

He died for me. As much as you and my family love me, none of you can save me, and I can't say no to Him just because you want me to."

I paused. She stayed silent, but I could tell she was listening. "Mom, if I were to die tomorrow and stand in front of God, you cannot come in and say 'please let her in, she's my daughter.' Roger can't come in and say 'please let her in, she's my wife.' No one can intercede for me. The only one who can intercede for me is Jesus Christ. So, I am a Christian. And no one can keep me from being that."

God definitely spoke through me that day. I was still pretty scared to say what I did, but I felt confidence flowing through me that I know came from the Holy Spirit. My mom didn't say anything after that and just changed the subject, but I had such joy and peace that I was finally able to start sharing my faith with her.

After this conversation, I gradually started talking more about God in my conversations with my family. My primary way of witnessing was not with words, but by letting my actions speak. But over time, I slowly interjected my faith into our conversations the more confident I grew. It was normally just a brief mention of something, like how we were going to do an activity at church that week, or how God had blessed us in a certain way.

A Bible verse I thought about often while I was growing the confidence to share my faith with my family was Matthew 10:33, where Jesus says that "whoever denies me before men, I also will deny before my Father who is in heaven." (ESV) I desperately did not want to deny my Father; I knew I owed my life to Him. I remember praying all the time for the strength to be bold so that I could tell my family about Jesus.

Initially, they ignored my comments about my new faith and moved on. But as the years passed and they saw this was a real thing that had completely changed my life, they accepted it. Now, they'll ask us how church went or what we're doing at church this week and it's a normal topic of conversation.

A few months after Zech was born, I told Roger I was done having babies. Not after 22 hours of labor and the pain I went through that day. Of course, I loved our son very much and deep in my heart had always wanted two kids, so when Roger said, "you know, it would be so good if we had a little girl. Then you'd have your dream, and she'll look just like you," it wasn't too hard to convince me. I also thought about how I had grown up with no siblings close to my age and knew that I needed to try to have another baby so my son wouldn't have to do that too.

We decided to try again, and 22 months later on June 1st, 2008, we welcomed our sweet Priscilla. Despite a scheduled c-section, she arrived a week before her due date. It was a Sunday, and Roger had taken Zech to church while I was at home by myself. I was "nesting," cleaning and organizing every room in preparation for our baby's arrival.

I started getting little cramps that slowly got bigger and stronger and thought, *Ooh, this doesn't feel right*. I called a friend and asked her to please get Roger and tell him to come home; he didn't have his phone on him at church. He came home, got me to the hospital and an hour later I had the c-section and Priscilla was here! As soon as I heard her sweet cry, I was in love. Roger put her next to my head while the doctors sewed me up, and I remember crying tears of joy looking at her beautiful face.

Roger's parents and sister helped us so much, which was a huge blessing. My mom and sisters came in July as soon as the school year was over. Priscilla was such a happy baby and is still such a happy girl. She smiles so much, people ask me if she ever gets sad or upset. Both of my children's love for the Lord is a beautiful thing for me to see; they both shine His light so well.

Those first years with them were definitely tough. With them being only 22 months apart, the diapers, breastfeeding and potty training felt endless at times. That first year after Priscilla was born when I was so exhausted trying to keep up with them and the house chores, I remember thinking, *What in the world did I do? What was I thinking having two kids so close together?* I couldn't always take care of myself the way that I wanted, and it was hard to make myself available to my husband. I was never depressed during this time, but certainly overwhelmed. However, as soon as Priscilla was about a year old and she and Zech started playing together, I was so glad we had them so close to each other. Their bond is strong, and it was beautiful to see it grow day by day as they got older.

Something unexpected I grappled with during those early years of having kids was the amount of worry I had for them. Of course, I knew before having kids that it was a huge responsibility, but you don't really understand what that means until you experience it. Having these two precious little lives in my hands to take care of brought me so much joy but also so much anxiety.

Being a mother is probably both the hardest thing I've ever done in my life and the most important thing I've ever done in my life. I remember worrying about every little thing, like *are they eating right? Are they growing like they should? Are they going to make it through the night?* I had heard of infant crib death, which terrified me; I woke up many nights to check on Zecharia and Priscilla to make sure they were both still alive and sleeping soundly.

Roger was helpful and understanding during this season of our lives. He was patient with me and listened to how I was feeling. One of my close friends who I met through church, Julie, was also a big encouragement to me as a new mom. She has two girls close in age to my kids but a little older, so she was able to give me lots of advice and help as I navigated the challenges of pregnancy and motherhood. She is my best friend to this day, and I count it a great blessing to be able to walk through life with her.

Worry is still something I struggle with, but it drives me to the best source of comfort available, my heavenly Father. He is always present, always peaceful. I found that if I use my anxiety about my kids and the busyness of our life as an excuse to not be as intentional in my relationship with Him, my anxiety only increases. I have to be intentional about spending time with Him and about staying encouraged in my community.

Roger used to travel every once in a while for his job, and on those Sundays I wouldn't go to church—I told myself that it was too much for me to take the kids by myself. After a couple years of this, I remember one day praying about something I was worried about and I felt conviction from the Holy Spirit: *Karima, going to church and being encouraged is not just a family thing. It's a personal choice.*

It was then that my relationship with God started to become more my own, individual and personal. I realized I needed that community of believers as much as possible, and began going to church whenever I could. Making church a priority was never a regret, and I could see my worry fading the more I was in God's Word.

Another struggle for me during those early years with kids was my independence. Even though I had two beautiful babies at home that I loved, I felt like I was losing myself and had a hard time not bringing home a paycheck. Especially as someone who had struggled with self-confidence my whole life, I felt I wasn't worth as much anymore. Even though I trusted Roger to provide for our family, it was still difficult putting myself in the vulnerable position of being a stay-at-home mom.

I clearly remember thinking, *What about my dreams? What about what I want?* I felt like I was missing out on doing things for myself or for my career, and I battled with that feeling for a while.

It felt like I was giving up all my control and fully depending on God and Roger to take care of me. I realized that being independent and working was another thing I had clung to as my identity, especially after my divorce. Being good at my job was something I could and should be proud of, but it was also something that I had made too important. God took everything I held onto for comfort other than Him—smoking, dressing up, working—and slowly took them away, showing me that my true fulfillment and joy and freedom could only be found in Him.

As I struggled to come to grips with my choice to stay home, I looked for books, videos or stories of other women to encourage me in what I was doing. I remember doing an internet search for "what does God think about a woman who stays home?" I came across Proverbs 31, a whole chapter in the Bible about the standard for a godly woman. She took care of her home and family first, while also having a business on the side, which encouraged me that I had made a good choice for my family.

I also found a blog post where the author articulated her thoughts on a godly stay-at-home mom that stuck with me. She said that if God had blessed you with the ability to stay at home with your children, think of it as a precious gift. To be able to see your babies grow up, crawl for the first time, take their first step, say their first word—these are milestones that don't come around twice. She asked, "Do you really want to give all those wonderful moments to a stranger?" Not all women are able to enjoy the luxury of time with their babies, and when I thought about it like that I realized what a treasure it was to be present with them.

Her article resonated with me deeply and included a lot of Scripture to back up her points. Roger was so encouraging during this time as well, and I remember him saying to me, "Karima, you know that Proverbs 31 woman? That is you." I took comfort in the fact that this time with my babies was a season in life, and God had me there with them to help them be happy, healthy, obedient children.

Looking back, it was of course God's timing and ironic sense of humor that had me living out surrender in my daily life just after I had really learned what it meant and surrendered fully to Him. This was yet another aspect of my life that I needed to give to Him, and I'm so glad that He walked me through every step. Our culture tells women we need to be independent and working to be successful, but sometimes God has other plans and different callings that are no less meaningful, and sometimes more so.

This stage of life also continued to grow mine and Roger's relationship. We became more of a team; I think parenting either forges your marriage stronger or it can break it apart. I'm so thankful that for us, it helped us learn to work together. Roger worked all day to support our family, and I took care of the kids and our home all day to support our family. We each couldn't do what we do without the other.

I am so grateful for Roger, who is my greatest encourager. He truly is perfect for me, and pushes me to be better as a follower of Jesus and as a woman, mom and entrepreneur. He's told me so many times that "whatever makes you happy, I want to do." I am abundantly blessed by him every day.

Shortly after Priscilla was born, we realized my hair salon wasn't running well without me. I couldn't put enough time into it to make it profitable, so unfortunately, we ended up selling it. I was sad, but knew I could always get back into the business and start again if I wanted to later. I felt bad for my customers, too. I had a great network of relationships and still do with many of my old customers. I'll bump into old customers to this day and they'll ask me when I'm coming back to cutting hair. My only regret with my customers is that I had been more bold in my faith at that time of my life. Now, it's hard for me to have a conversation with someone without talking about Jesus. But back then, I was still so young in my faith that I didn't really talk about Him that much, and now I wish I had taken more opportunities to share His love with all the people I came in contact with through my business.

Once the business was sold, my full-time job became the kids and our home. Not being someone who likes to sit still, I volunteered a lot at church, helped Roger with some administrative things with his business and volunteered at the kids' school as soon as they started going. During this season was when Roger went back to school and got his MBA. He worked so hard, and I was so proud of him. I was truly living out the role of being his helpmate, taking care of everything at home so that he could excel at his role in providing for us.

I remember having moments during the early years with the kids where I thought, *I never saw myself here, as this person. My role is literally to serve my family in all their needs.* But I truly wouldn't have it any other way. I had a driving force awaken in me after we had kids. I love my family so much and get such satisfaction from serving them, and wouldn't want anyone else doing the things I get to do for them.

As the kids got older, I looked for opportunities to serve with them, to teach them the value of serving others to serve the Lord. In 2010, I got involved with a nonprofit organization called GLOW (God Loves Orphans & Widows) run by a lady from my church. She and her husband started GLOW because of a heartbreaking experience they had, where the adoption of a little boy into their family ultimately fell through at the last hour. In an effort to serve the orphans and widows in their local community, they started GLOW. They give out clothes, food and other necessities to orphans and widows, as well as run different events throughout the year to help support them.

I started serving with her at their Thanksgiving village every November, which I still love doing to this day. She has all the volunteers dress up as a pilgrim or Indian, and we help give away all types of food for Thanksgiving dinner, from turkeys, to canned cranberry sauce and sweet potatoes, for families who can't afford to purchase special food for Thanksgiving.

I also had the opportunity to start a nursing home ministry, taking my kids with me as soon as they could walk. We went to our local nursing home, brought the residents goodies and just sat and talked with them. Many of them didn't have families who would come visit often, and they absolutely loved seeing us, especially the kids. Watching Zech and Priscilla interact with them was so heartwarming to witness, and I loved how I could teach my kids to love those who needed it most, the way God loves us.

That year, we also encountered some of our first losses as a family—Roger's father and my grandmother in Morocco passed away. A couple of years later, we also lost my grandmother in France, Roger's mother, and Roger's son. Although each of these losses were difficult and we still miss them dearly, it was bittersweet to see how our faith grew as we watched the Lord carry us through each loss. We could see His hand so clearly comforting us and holding us up. We are also still blessed to have Roger's son's wife and kids with us. Between his older son and daughter, we have five wonderful grandkids.

My grandmother's passing hit me hard—we were literally planning a trip to Morocco that year so she could meet the kids, her first great-grandchildren. The kids' pediatrician warned against taking them to Africa too young, which is why we had waited until 2010 when Priscilla was two. We had visited France in 2007 when Zech was one, but I was heartbroken that they missed meeting my grandmother.

I also had regrets that I never shared my faith with my grandmother before she passed. Even though Roger and I had made some great memories with her and the rest of the family on our two visits to Morocco together, I was still scared of her.

She was in full control of her house until the day she died, controlling all conversations and interactions. When we visited, it seemed like she was everywhere, so we didn't talk about much in front of her. If someone started a conversation and she didn't understand what we were talking about, she'd snap, "Hey! What are you talking about?" Our only "free" time when she was alive was still during her afternoon naps. Even as adults we would all sneak upstairs to chat and hang out.

Calling was also very expensive for a long time, and even when she got a phone in the house in the early 2000s, she was the only one who was allowed to answer the phone. I couldn't call my other family members and talk to them until after she passed.

I remember one time I called her when I was about five months pregnant with Zech; we had just sent her money, and I wanted to make sure she received it. After Roger and I were together and financially stable, I tried to send them money once or twice a year to help them out. It wasn't much, but a little goes a long way over there. I always sent the money to her (now I can send it to my aunts and uncles, but when she was alive, if anyone else received anything she'd open it and take it regardless). It was exactly like when my mom used to send me gifts when I lived there as a little girl.

She also would never call us—we had to call her. So I called her from work that day, expecting her to be thankful and happy for what we sent. When she picked up, I said, "Hey, *moue*, I sent you some money—did you get it?"

"Oh, so *now* you're sending me money? *Now* you're calling me?" she snapped. "You ungrateful girl, just leaving me to die over here all alone." She went on for a minute or two, and finally I was able to get off the phone, in tears. I'm sure my pregnancy hormones had something to do with my emotional response, but I was hoping she would be happy and thank me, and instead the words she said broke my heart. It was a rude awakening that she was still the same person she had always been, and a part of me still craved acceptance from her until the day she died.

She probably would have freaked out if I told her I wasn't a Muslim anymore, and at the time I was still terrified of her disapproval. Now, I'm a completely different person through Christ's strength, but I wish I had the confidence to share Jesus with her back then. I also wish I could tell her now that the way she treated us was not right.

We still got to visit Morocco that year, and it was wonderful getting to show Zecharia and Priscilla off to the rest of the family. Roger brought his Bible, and one night we started talking to the rest of the family about religion. They knew since he was American that he probably wasn't Muslim, so they tried to explain more about Islam, and we got to share about Jesus and Christianity with them. We went back and forth and had a long conversation about it, but they listened to my whole testimony and were okay that I was no longer Muslim. I was so grateful that night that God gave us the opportunity and confidence to share with them. Now, I try to talk with them and share my faith more often. I also believe that my actions can sometimes even be a better way to witness to them, and I pray that as they see the changes in my life, seeds are being planted in their hearts.

On that visit, I did find a deeper appreciation for my grandmother and her home than I ever had before. She had been insistent on always keeping her house so that her children could have a place to all come together; she really enjoyed having everyone together. She got many offers over the years from people wanting to buy the house, one even for a half million dollars, but she always said no. I remember her saying, "I'm not selling my house to anyone. I'm keeping it for my kids."

Being there with all my family that summer, I realized that despite her abuse, she loved and cared for her family deeply; she just never knew how to show us. Now, every time we visit Morocco we stay at my childhood home, where my unmarried aunts and uncle still live today. Despite her flaws, my grandmother instilled in each of us the importance of family, for which I'll be forever grateful.

Chapter 21

The Silent Rupture

And we know that in all things God works for the good of those who love him, who have been called according to his purpose. —Romans 8:28

Once Priscilla was done breastfeeding, I was unhappy with the way my body looked. Even though my self-esteem had grown by leaps and bounds, especially as I grew as a Christian, becoming a busy mom left me feeling like I needed a confidence boost. I wasn't able to go out much anymore or practice self-care, so I started thinking about getting my implants redone.

Roger was supportive, so I found a surgeon in Savannah to do the procedure. I had the surgery after our Morocco trip in 2010, when Priscilla was two, so Roger's older sister, Mitzi, came and stayed with us to help take care of the family while I recovered.

Mitzi is another sister to me, and has been amazing when we've needed help through the years. She knows I'm the caregiver of our family, and is always willing to come visit and jump in wherever is needed, no questions asked. She's a little older than Roger and all her children were teenagers when Roger and I got married, so by the time I was having kids, hers were all out of the house. She is a selfless human being, and she and her husband have been such wonderful blessings to us many times.

Around Christmas in 2015, I started noticing some hardness in my left breast and experiencing some other health issues. I was tired all the time, and started having pain in my lower abdomen. I thought I had some sort of infection, and went to my OBGYN several times to be tested. Each time, they would come back and say, "No, there's nothing wrong with you." But I was still hurting.

Then, I started having a burning sensation down my left side, all the way down into my leg. I thought I could be having back or nerve problems, so I went to a spine doctor, who also said I had nothing wrong with me. He tested my nerves and muscles in some very painful tests, but still could find nothing wrong.

Over the next few months, I started having tachycardia and out of the blue my heart rate would skyrocket. I went to a cardiologist and walked on their treadmill, did stress tests and even a heart ultrasound—but there was nothing wrong with my heart. I was getting a sensation of pins and needles all over my body, and even my hair started thinning. I remember when someone asked me if I had gotten my hair cut; I didn't realize until then how much I had lost.

My life gradually became all about doctors and appointments. I was constantly in pain, unable to function normally. I eventually went back to my implant surgeon, who said my left side did feel a little hard, but that was normal. He said sometimes a little blood gets in between the implant and the skin, which can create hard spots and scar tissue. He explained that sometimes the scar tissue can become calcified and thick if your body has a reaction to the foreign object inside. He gave me some medicine and told me to gently massage the area to see if that would help.

Later that day, I decided to try massaging the area at home. Almost immediately, my body started burning with heat, mostly on the left side. In tears, I thought, *What is wrong with me? Why can't I just be normal again?* Little did I know I was actually pushing toxins from the implant into my body with every massage. It took me a while to connect the implants to the pain I was feeling, because I didn't want to think they could be the cause.

It became more difficult to stand in the shower. My feet would get really tingly, like all my nerve endings were going crazy. Sometimes it was more like a burning sensation, like I had ants biting my feet.

I tried running on the treadmill—Roger thought maybe I could work out the pain. Every time I started to run, it felt like thousands of ants were biting all up and down my legs; it was the weirdest feeling and so painful. As soon as I'd start walking again, the feeling would go away. My head would randomly start spinning some days, and I would have to lie down until the feeling went away. This myriad of symptoms affected my whole body for two years.

Eventually, Roger gently suggested, "Honey, maybe there's nothing wrong with you." I knew he felt helpless, watching me in constant discomfort and pain. But I knew something was wrong—this wasn't how I was supposed to be feeling every day. The pain started affecting me mentally, and I had days where I was very depressed. After I would drop the kids off at school, it was all I could do to get home and lie down, which was not like my active, busy, normal self at all.

Some days I had to lie in bed for hours on end, unable to get up or my heart rate would skyrocket. Not being able to get up and care for my husband and kids or be present with them was frustrating, but they all encouraged me and helped me with whatever I needed.

I was constantly exhausted and in pain, and I couldn't get away from it. If I had listened to all the doctors I saw, I would have been on all sorts of medications, from heart and nerve pain meds to anti-anxiety meds. But I knew those medications would just be masking the symptoms, not the root cause, and I desperately wanted answers.

Outwardly, I looked healthy, and nothing showed up in any of my lab work or tests. It started to make me feel crazy; I did a lot of crying those two years. Roger would come home from work and see the pain I was in, and would feel so bad for me. But he also felt helpless to fix whatever was wrong.

However, that season of struggle brought me close to God in ways I couldn't have imagined. I did a lot of praying and reading my Bible, looking for comfort in the pages of God's Word. I remember one day I came across Psalm 139:14, which says, "I praise you, for I am fearfully and wonderfully made. Wonderful are your works; my soul knows it very well." (ESV)

At that point, I had googled my symptoms and found women who had many of my same issues because of their breast implants, but I didn't want to believe it. After reading that verse, I finally acknowledged, *maybe my implants are the problem. Maybe I need to seriously think about taking them out.* I had a mammogram before this to check, but it showed no ruptures in the implants. The only other way to check them would be to take them out.

It was such a hard decision. I had lived with implants for so long, and didn't realize how much self-esteem I had tied to them until I thought about getting them out. I was scared of what I would look like. The best encouragement to me as I made my decision besides God's Word was of course, Roger. I remember him saying, "Honey, I don't care what you look like. I can see the pain in your face every day—we just want you healthy again."

I had my first implants to get the approval of others and afterward had made them a part of my identity. I think many women tend to do that—find value in our appearance. But the more I thought and prayed about it, God spoke to my heart: *Karima, I already made you perfect and just the way I want you to be! You don't have to do anything to your body to earn my approval because I already made you in My image.*

With Roger echoing that truth to me, I slowly realized how I had been holding on to the way I looked and presented myself as an idol. Dressing modestly was only the beginning of necessary change in my life; I needed to give this area to God too. I realized how my identity couldn't be in my cup size—it had to be in Christ and His promises, things that would never change.

In February 2017, I finally went in for the removal surgery. I had another mammogram a week before, but still was told nothing was wrong with the implants. However, after opening me up, they found the left implant ruptured and leaking its yellow, gooey insides into my body. My energy came back almost immediately after surgery, and most of my other symptoms went away quickly too. I could feel the burning sensation gone as soon as I woke up from surgery. I still deal with some health issues from the implants today, for example, my body throbs after cutting Roger's hair for fifteen minutes in our bathroom.

But I am so grateful that what I deal with now is nowhere near as horrible as what I went through those two years.

I learned a valuable lesson through that experience—if your identity is in Christ, you feel complete. No matter what happens, I try to put my confidence in the Lord and remember that my body is just a temporary shell. The culture tells us we need so many things to be happy or beautiful, and it's all lies and a waste of time. I learned that all the energy I had been spending on earthly things would be better spent on eternal things.

After I recovered from surgery, I became more involved in the lives of others. Instead of comparing myself to others, I looked for opportunities to help them. Slowly, I gained confidence with sharing the gospel. Struggling with my self-esteem made me hyper-focused on myself. Thoughts like, *oh my gosh, what does so-and-so think about me,* or *do I look good enough* used to float through my head constantly. Now, my life is more about what I can do to serve others.

Someone from my past who I was able to share the gospel with was my childhood friend, Aude, from France. We had stayed in contact through the years, sending cassette tapes we recorded back and forth across the globe and visiting while I was with family in France. Eventually, we connected on social media and I found out she had terminal cancer. I felt compelled to share my hope and faith with her, and we were able to have many wonderful conversations about it. By what she said in her last message to me before she passed, I think she did accept Christ, and I look forward to seeing her again someday in heaven.

God helped me realize that I would never be enough for the world. I had always wanted to be different, ever since I was a little girl in France wishing for blonde hair and blue eyes. But He has made each one of us perfect, and when we try to change ourselves we are changing God's perfect creation, which is not our job. This was yet another thing I had to give up to become more like Christ; another thing I had been holding on to as a way to express my "freedom" as a woman, when, in fact, giving it up gave me more freedom than I had ever felt before.

The most fulfilling part of my growth in this area has been seeing my beautiful daughter living out her life so confident in her identity in Christ. Being able to teach her from my mistakes and watch her make better choices is the best gift. Her childlike faith encourages me every day to continue living for Him.

Chapter 22

Transforming Grace

For we are God's handiwork, created in Christ Jesus to do good works, which God prepared in advance for us to do.
—Ephesians 2:10

As I slowly learned to give up control of my life to the Lord, another area I felt conviction from the Holy Spirit about was alcohol. I wasn't drinking on a regular basis, just having a glass of wine occasionally or when Roger and I would get to go out, but this nagging feeling that I needed to stop wouldn't go away. I had started drinking in my early twenties, and I realized it was a comfort for me during all those dark years of abuse.

No one encouraged me in my attempts to quit drinking except Roger. My friends would ask, "Why? It's not like you're getting drunk or even drinking all the time. What's the harm?" But when I brought it up with Roger, he said, "Honey, if you're convicted about it, you should stop." He wasn't convicted about it, so while we quit smoking together, quitting drinking was something I did on my own.

I tried time and time again, but every time I failed. I didn't think it was going to be as hard to quit as it was. But when everyone around me was saying, "It's not that bad," or it was being offered everywhere I went out, I couldn't say no. That's when I realized how much I was holding onto it, as well as how much I wanted to overcome it. But as I continued to fail to accomplish my goal, I was slowly confronted with the reality that this wasn't something I could do in my own strength. The Holy Spirit convicted me—I needed to rely on God for the strength to let this thing go.

As the kids got older, I remember them asking me what I was drinking when I had a glass of wine, and I would lie and tell them it was juice. I always felt so guilty when that would happen. I didn't want to be hiding anything from my kids and setting that kind of example. I was also in the midst of many health issues due to my breast implants and knew it would probably be best for my heart and overall health to stop drinking.

I also had an experience where I felt that drinking impacted my ability to share the gospel. We were on vacation, and I was chatting with another couple at the resort while my husband was off playing with the kids. As we talked, I mentioned something about how the Lord had blessed me, and the couple didn't say anything. Usually, Christians respond to something like that in a way that indicates their faith, so I assumed this couple did not know the Lord.

I felt like I had an opportunity to share the gospel with them, but because I had a drink in my hand, I was embarrassed and felt like I couldn't. I didn't think drinking while sharing the gospel was the best representation of Christ. After the fact, I was so disappointed in myself and was convicted even more strongly to quit drinking, because I never wanted to feel ashamed to share my faith.

But all of these perfectly good reasons weren't good enough to really stop the habit. After several months of trying on my own and failing, I went to my Bible, desperately searching for some kind of encouragement. I looked up every verse about drinking, being drunk, and the consequences of those choices. My personal conviction after that research was that drinking wasn't necessarily wrong—being drunk certainly was—but it could easily tempt a person in the wrong direction.

One specific passage that really spoke to me during this time was Titus 2:3-4, which says, "Older women likewise are to be reverent in behavior, not slanderers or slaves to too much wine. They are to teach what is good, and so train the young women to love their husbands and children."

I went back to those verses as reminders daily, praying for God's help. I realized that if I was really going to stop drinking, it had to be a decision between me and the Lord. Going back to the Bible really helped me break that sin—and it was a sin for me. It was something I was holding onto for my flesh that I didn't want to surrender to the Lord. I had to learn over my many failures that life choices honoring God aren't about pleasing the people around you or succumbing to peer pressure.

This was yet another thing God used in my life to break the mold of my flesh and make me more like Him. Growing up, my life was all about making sure others were okay, whether it was my grandmother, aunts and uncles or my mom. After that, it was about trying to make my ex-husband happy, which led me to trying to make myself happy. When that didn't satisfy me, I was still as lost and lonely as that little Moroccan girl.

I am eternally grateful that God didn't stop pursuing me, and now my goal in life is to please Him—the most fulfilling choice I could ever make. As I struggled to give up alcohol, I remember reflecting on all this and thinking, *So, Karima. You mean to tell me that Jesus came down to this earth, was beaten, crucified and died, paying for your sins on the cross, and you can't stop this one thing? Really?*

As I thought more about that, it resonated with me—Jesus gave everything for me, so I could give up this one thing for Him. Don't get me wrong, it was still a battle after that! I even had dreams about having a drink, which was so funny to me because I didn't crave alcohol, I just didn't want to have to say no to it. Now, I haven't had a drink in almost ten years. Roger tells me I'm so strong, but I say it's not true—I know it's not in my strength, and I don't even know how I'm doing it. It's all for the Lord.

This was just another thing on the list of things I used to do, things that I thought made me who I was and gave me my freedom. But God slowly, gently, patiently turned me towards Him. *You don't need that control anymore, my daughter. Give it to me. Depend on me. Trust me. Be satisfied in me—I will bless you beyond measure and give you all you need.*

The longer I live as a Christian, the more I learn that surrender isn't a one time decision, but a lifelong one, as I painfully shed my flesh to be more like Christ. I am a sinner in need of God's grace, and becoming more like Him is a daily fight against my flesh; but one where He is with me, every step of the way.

One of the most gratifying parts of my faith journey has been watching my kids choose Christianity for themselves. Ever since they could read and understand, Roger and I did devotionals with them in the mornings before school. One morning when they were in elementary school, our devotional was based on Hebrews 12:1, which says, "Let us run the race with endurance that God has set before us." After Roger had finished reading, Zech asked, "So, Daddy, the race starts when we are born?" I remember Roger smiled and explained. "That is a good guess son, but no. The race starts when we ask Jesus into our hearts."

Zech thought about that for a minute, then out of the blue said, "Well then, I want Jesus in my heart!" I remember exchanging a quick glance with Roger as my eyes filled with tears, and I could see that he was thinking the same thing I was–*this is amazing!* We prayed with him right there, and he accepted Jesus into his heart. Then Priscilla said, "I want Jesus in my heart too!" Tears started escaping my eyes as we prayed with her right then, too. On my way to drop them off at school that day, Priscilla just kept saying over and over, "I have Jesus in my heart!" with a huge smile on her face.

They asked us about getting baptized soon after that. We talked as a family about what baptism meant and how important it was for it to be a personal conviction, not something that is done just because mom and dad did it. We also went to our pastor about it, and did a lot of studying and talking with the kids to make sure they understood their salvation and how baptism would be a public declaration of that to our church.

Two years later, in 2018, Roger baptized them both at our church. I was so proud of them, and reflected that day how thankful I was that God had saved not only me and Roger, but also our kids, and that we got to witness them declaring their salvation publicly. Zecharia even got up in front of the whole church and shared a short testimonial message from him and Priscilla. He said, "Hello, my name is Zecharia and this is my little sister Priscilla. A couple of years ago me and my family were doing our devotional like we do every day. But that day was different. After the lesson, me and my sister asked our parents if we could accept God into our hearts and they said yes. So that day, me and my sister accepted Christ. And now we are here today to be baptized to show that we love Jesus and we want to obey him. We also want to share a verse with you all. Galatians 3:27 says 'For all you who were baptized into Christ have clothes yourselves with Christ.' Thank you!" It was such a sweet speech from him, and a memorable day for our family.

As the kids grew older and started high school, I found myself with less and less on my plate. I stayed involved in their school and in church, but as they became more independent, I was starting to have more time on my hands. Both Roger and the kids had been encouraging me for years to share my testimony publicly in some way, with videos or by writing a book. The kids would always say, "Mom, you have such an amazing story to tell!" I always responded by saying I was too busy, but as my responsibilities with the kids started to fall away, I felt the Holy Spirit tugging on my heart to start sharing how God had changed my life. I knew I had a story to tell, I just didn't know where to even start.

Every time I shared with someone a little bit about my testimony, they would say, "Wow! You need to write a book!" I found myself wishing I could find someone who could just write a book for me. For several years, I researched off and on about how to start up a YouTube channel and how to write a book; I probably could have written a book with all the notes I took! But I couldn't seem to muster up the courage to do either one.

I went to many different church events and women's conferences where I'd hear the different speakers sharing from the Bible or talking about their own personal life experiences, and I always felt this urge to get up there and talk about all that God had done for me! But every time that thought would come up, it was followed by so many of the devil's lies: *You're not educated enough to get up in front of people and talk! Who do you think you are? Your story doesn't really matter—it wouldn't impact anyone. No one is going to want to hear it. You are a nobody.*

I let those lies and my own fears hold me back for so long. We joined a new church in 2019, and the pastor there, Pastor Cam, really stuck out to me. He spoke in such a relaxed way, like he was just chatting with friends, when he was actually preaching to thousands of people. I remember sitting in church one Sunday and thinking, *if this guy can get up and talk in front of all these people and just talk to them like friends, I can maybe do that too.* I realized I didn't have to use any fancy words, just speak from the heart.

The COVID lockdown in 2020 ended up being the perfect time for me to overcome my fears and get started. Since the kids were doing school at home, we had a lot of free time together. Zech came to me and said, "Mom, this is the time. If you want to start a YouTube channel, I'm home and can help you get it going." I said okay, and we got started. He was amazing—he learned how to use a software program to edit videos and taught me how to use it. Roger had some backgrounds, stands and lighting equipment from one of his business ventures, so I was able to use his stuff to start out.

We have a mother-in-law suite in our house, so I got everything all set up in there. I remember the first day I set up my phone to start recording; it was just me in the room, but I was still nervously sweating! But that day, my YouTube channel "LifeChat with Karima" was born.

My first video was about my breast implants, since that whole story was fresh on my mind. As I started to get more

TRANSFORMING GRACE | 175

comfortable, I did videos on all the different parts of my life—my faith, my health issues, abusive relationships and more. The videos did well, and I began receiving responses from my viewers, people all over the world thanking me for sharing my stories and helping them in their faith journeys. It was so encouraging to see how God could use my trials to help others and bring Him glory. I even got invited to do a few interviews with different podcasts, where I've been able to reach even more people with my story and the hope I've received from Christ.

Now today, I have over a thousand followers, and most of the people who have liked my testimony video are from India and Pakistan. It's crazy to look back and see how God has blessed my little, scared step of faith. I get to share the gospel with so many people worldwide now, and all the glory goes to Him.

Another huge blessing that came out of starting to share my stories on YouTube is that my family in France and Morocco can see everything that I post, especially my younger cousins who are more tech savvy. It has become another way that I can share my faith with them without me even having direct conversation with them. I am so blessed that my family all respect and accept my decision to be a Christian, as I know many Muslims who are disowned by their families when they leave Islam for another religion. I love my family so much, and I pray every day that God would soften their hearts and that one day, they would accept Jesus.

Chapter 23

Runaway Heart

"I have told you these things, so that in me you may have peace. In this world you will have trouble. But take heart! I have overcome the world." —John 16:33

Ever since I had my breast implants removed, I've done everything I could possibly do to be healthy and heal my body. Most of my symptoms went away, but one of the scariest ones stuck around and would flare up every once in a while, and that was my tachycardia. Sometimes, when bending down to pick up my purse, my heart rate would shoot up to 250. It happened in the most random places—lying by the pool relaxing on vacation, in WalMart while I was grocery shopping, setting something down at the gym; there didn't seem to be a pattern or reason.

Normally, the episodes would last anywhere from a few minutes to an hour. But as the year progressed after my surgery, they started lasting several hours to overnight, and Roger and I started to become worried again.

I tried going to the emergency room a few times, but every time I went, my heart rate would slow down back to normal before they took my pulse. I also saw a cardiologist regularly, and he did all the tests, including stress tests, EKGs and ultrasounds, but saw nothing. One time he even sent me home with a heart monitoring system for a week, but I never had an episode that whole time. He put me on beta blockers, but those weren't stopping the attacks either.

He mentioned at one point how he had a patient with heart problems due to breast implants before, but when she had them removed her symptoms went away. I was a mystery to him, because I was having episodes on a regular basis, but never when a doctor could catch them in action. It was terrifying for me; I felt like my heart was a ticking time bomb, and I never knew when it was about to go off.

The worst episode I ever had happened at the worst possible time, when Roger's mother passed away. The evening of her viewing, my heart rate jumped up over 250, and it took almost 20 hours for it to come back down. I had to go home and lie down, and as I lay there I remember feeling so hopeless and scared. I tried everything I was told could help, from putting my face in ice water to laying with my feet up against a wall, and nothing would help. I finally fell asleep that night, heart thumping, hoping it would go down in the night.

But the next morning, I woke up and it was still going nonstop. I really wanted to go to my mother-in-law's funeral that day and be there for Roger, so I felt like a trip to the emergency room would be a waste of time. I just hoped and prayed it would stop soon. It had never gone on that long before, so I desperately hoped that it would stop any minute.

By the time we were supposed to leave for the funeral that afternoon, my heart was still racing. I tearfully told Roger that I was so sorry, but he needed to go without me. Of course, he didn't make me feel worse, but as I lay in my bed crying, I felt horrible not being able to be the supportive wife I wanted to be.

I remember getting on Facebook and posting to ask for prayers. A friend of mine saw the post and reached out to me, telling me to try a specific breathing technique to see if it would help. At that point, I felt like I'd been running on a treadmill for twenty hours; I was exhausted, cold, tired and ready to try anything. Within minutes of trying the technique, my heart rate started to slow and quickly went back to normal.

I threw my black dress on as quickly as I could, slapped some makeup on and drove straight to the funeral home. I was still white as a ghost, so when I walked in halfway through the service people could tell something was wrong, but I didn't care—I just wanted to be with Roger and support him in his grief.

After the funeral, I went home and rested. It took me about a week to fully recover from that episode. Roger suggested I try a different cardiologist, to see if he could see something my first one couldn't. So I found a different cardiologist, went in for an appointment and explained what had been going on all the way up through the latest episode. He did a few tests, then told me to wait while he looked at the results. After a few minutes, he came back in and said, "You need to leave my office now—you've just completely wasted my time. There is nothing wrong with you!"

Crushed, I left his office in tears. No medical professional would believe me, since they could never see my symptoms for themselves. Finally, at an appointment with my original cardiologist, he suggested buying a device called a Kardia, which is a mobile EKG monitor that would enable me to take my EKG at home. I wasted no time ordering one, and by God's grace that very week I had another episode and was able to finally record my EKG while it was happening and send it to my cardiologist.

Afterwards, I went in for another appointment, and he was able to see the problem with my heart and refer me to a surgeon for a catheter ablation. He said the cause could have been something I was born with, or something that happened as I got older. I am fairly certain that the silicone from my breast implants exacerbated the problem.

While I was elated to finally know what was wrong and how to fix it, I was also scared to have any procedure done on my heart. However, I knew that if I didn't have it, my episodes would keep happening and impact my health down the road. I was also anxious to try to get my quality of life back. Roger and I prayed a lot about it, and we both had peace that having the procedure done was the right course of action.

So in February 2021, I went in and had the ablation. It was just a one day procedure—I was awake but under sedation, so thankfully, I don't remember any of it. The surgeon took a catheter and threaded it up from my groin area toward my heart and used it to burn the damaged area of my heart.

It took a few months for me to fully recover, but once I was healed I never had another tachycardia episode again. To this day, when I do something exciting or scary I can still feel a tiny twinge, like my heart wants to do something, but thankfully it never does.

Once I made it past all the heart issues and was healthy again, I felt like the Lord was leading me to continue being bold and sharing my story more. I had been sharing on my YouTube channel for over a year at this point, but I felt the Holy Spirit tugging on my heart to do more.

At the beginning of 2022, a friend of mine, Marie, who went to a different church, reached out and asked if I would be willing to share my story and be the main speaker at a women's conference at their church. She said she had watched a lot of my YouTube videos and thought there would be many women who could relate to different parts of my testimony. Excited and terrified at the same time, I said yes.

I remember when I walked up on the stage that day, my legs were shaking as nervous thoughts rolled around in my head. *What are these ladies going to think of me? Will they like the way I look? What am I about to say?* I took a deep breath and said a quick prayer. *Father, let this be about you and not me. Speak through me.* I remember thinking, *Remember Karima, you're only talking to one person. One person out there needs to hear God's Word today. This is not about you—it's for the Lord.* As I started to talk, my confidence began to rise and my words flowed more naturally. I felt like I was just having a conversation with a friend, and I truly believe the Holy Spirit took over and spoke through me that day.

Although I had faced my fear of speaking in public, I still struggled with self-doubt when I thought about writing my story. I remember thinking, *Why should I think my story is unique? I'm sure people wouldn't be interested. It's not going to affect or help anyone.* Of course, these were just lies from the devil, but it was how I felt at the time.

Around the same time, our church recommended one Sunday that we watch the TV series "The Chosen" as families. My family and I have now watched every season multiple times—we just can't get enough of it! It has helped each of us deepen our personal relationships with the Lord as we've seen the Bible in action.

As I watched Jesus call each of His disciples one by one, I

saw how they were all imperfect sinners with obvious things in their lives that, by all appearances, would make them unsuitable for ministry. Some were disabled, not educated or poor, and yet they still left everything and everyone to follow Him. I realized that if Jesus called those people to serve Him and preach the gospel, surely He could use me too. I found such comfort in the thought that my imperfections and struggles were what qualified me to be used in a unique way by my Savior.

After that realization, I decided I would follow His guidance and write a book, but I wanted to continue working on my YouTube channel first and building my following there. I also realized that the more I was sharing, the more I felt the need to work on my own relationship with the Lord and grow and learn even more, so that I could stay strong in my faith. So, later that year, I joined a women's Bible study at my church. About sixteen of us meet every Thursday, and that time has been such a blessing in my life. When I joined, we started a book called *Becoming a Contagious Christian*, which was all about learning to share the gospel in an impactful way—exactly what I was looking to learn. God guided me right where I needed to be, and my sisters in Christ who I have met through that group have been and continue to be one of the biggest blessings in my life.

Of course, God knew what He was doing in not having me start my book right then and building up my support system in our church. Little did I know that my toughest trial yet was right around the corner.

Chapter 24

When Faith is All That Remains

Even though I walk through the darkest valley, I will fear no evil, for you are with me; your rod and your staff, they comfort me. —Psalm 23:4

In March of 2023, Priscilla was scheduled to go on a school trip to Myrtle Beach to perform as part of her theatre and chorus group, and I was asked to go along as a chaperon for the girls. It was going to be mine and Priscilla's first trip away from home together, and she was so excited.

Roger decided to plan something special for him and Zech while we were gone. His favorite hobby since the kids were born has been race car driving—he was invited by a friend back in 2007, and after his first drive, he was hooked. He started out driving at driver's education weekends, where you bring your own car and an instructor teaches you how to drive on the track. I've actually done those myself a few times, and they are so much fun. Roger picked up the techniques quickly, and he was a great driver. He started racing soon after learning and had been doing it ever since, at tracks all around the U.S. Naturally, he wanted to take Zech to the track and teach him how to drive, so they made plans to go on the Saturday of the weekend Priscilla and I were going on our trip. I have to admit, I was a little nervous, but I knew Roger was a safe, experienced driver and Zech would be in good hands.

They were both so excited—Roger even got Zech a helmet with his name on it. I have a picture of them both standing in our driveway in front of the car a few days before the weekend, smiling from ear to ear.

Priscilla and I left on a Friday morning with her school group, and they performed at the theatre in Myrtle Beach that night. They did an amazing job, and the next day, the plan was for all of us chaperons and students to head to the local aquarium, then a shopping area and then leave that afternoon to head back home.

That morning, Roger sent us a text that said "We just got to the track! We love you! Have a great day and see you soon." I responded, "You guys have a great day too! We love you so much." Priscilla and I had breakfast and then headed over to the aquarium with the rest of her group. Once we got there, the teacher started organizing the students and chaperons into smaller groups, and that is when I glanced at my phone and saw I had a missed call from Zech. I was about to call him back when I got a text from him that said, "Mom, please call me right away, there's an emergency."

I felt my heart drop to my toes when I read that. My mind was racing through all the possibilities in the seconds before I called him. *It's not Zech, because he's texting me. It has to be Roger. Oh dear Lord, be with us.* I told the teacher I needed to step away to call my son and that it was an emergency, and she said it was no problem, that they would wait for me before going in.

Zech answered right away, and my worst fears were confirmed. He was so calm, trying to be brave for me. "Mom, dad was in a very bad accident. He is bleeding internally, and he's in an ambulance about to go to the hospital right now." I felt my jaw drop; I couldn't believe what I was hearing. "Mom, someone is giving me a ride to the hospital, and we're following the ambulance to Savannah." I was in shock—I couldn't think of what to ask or what to say. "Mom, I'll call you as soon as we get there and give you an update." I don't even remember what I said. My mind went numb as he hung up the phone.

When I turned around, everyone in our group could tell by the look on my face that something was horribly wrong. "My husband was in a very bad accident," I said. My daughter's teacher was an amazing Christian woman, and right away she said, "Let's pray." Everyone gathered around me and Priscilla to pray for Roger. Afterwards, she told me to take all the time I needed and to let them know if there was anything they could do. The group went into the aquarium, and Priscilla and I found the closest bench and sat down, crying. I was in shock and my stomach was churning; I felt like I was going to throw up any minute. As I held my terrified daughter, trying to comfort her as tears streamed down my own face, I felt totally helpless. *Father God, please help Roger to be okay.*

Minutes later, I got another call from Zecharia. "Hey Mom, we made it to the hospital. Do you want to see Dad?" Of course I said yes, but inside I was terrified, not knowing what I was about to see. He turned our call into a FaceTime and I saw my sweet husband on a stretcher with a neck brace on, his face contorted as he moaned in pain. My body started shaking with uncontrollable sobs. Through our tears, Priscilla and I told him we loved him and were praying for him. He was in so much pain, I couldn't help but continue sobbing. I remember taking a few screenshots of the call, thinking this was the last time I'd see my husband alive. After a minute, Zech said, "I'm sorry mom, I have to hang up. Dad can hear you cry, it's hurting him." *Click.* My crying was making Roger cry, putting him in even more pain.

A few minutes later, one of the chaperons from our group came out to ask how things were going, and I told her we were still waiting for news. She kindly offered to take Priscilla inside to try to distract her a little bit. I told Priscilla to go ahead, and I'd update her as soon as I heard something.

As they walked away, the seriousness of the situation started to hit me. I think my body subconsciously realized it didn't have to try to hold my emotions together and put on a brave face for my daughter anymore. I felt myself falling to my knees, and I started bawling, makeup and tears streaming down my face.

It was not a pretty sight—the people coming in and out of the aquarium must have thought I was crazy or something. But I didn't care…all I could think about was that I might never see my husband again.

Once I was able to gather myself again a little bit, I decided to post a quick update on Facebook, asking people to pray for Roger. Almost immediately, hundreds of people were responding, and I started getting calls from friends asking if there was anything they could do. Some even offered to come get me. I realized having someone come get me wouldn't make sense, since by the time they got where I was I would be halfway back to Savannah on the bus. I even had one friend looking for a flight for us.

A dear friend of mine, Sarah, called and said "Karima, I'm about five minutes away from the hospital. I'm heading over right now to sit with Zecharia and make sure he's okay." She got him lunch and ended up staying there with him most of the day. Another friend, April, and her husband and son picked up Zech later in the day and took him back to the track to pick up all of his and Roger's things that got left behind. They dropped everything off at our house, bought Zech dinner and took him back to the hospital. I was beyond grateful for these and so many others who were able to help us that day.

Finally, Zech was able to call me back and show me Roger again. He said, "Mom, I will show you Dad, but you can't cry." I gathered myself as best as I could for those few minutes and tried to be as brave as my sweet son. At that point, he was able to give me an update and tell me the whole story of what had happened. He told me the doctors weren't sure what all the damage was yet, but Roger definitely had a broken back. *Oh my gosh, what if he never walks again?* I was so afraid for him, but kept praying every minute. It was crazy how in this most horrible time, I could still feel God's presence and peace comforting me.

Zech said when they arrived at the track, he had gone to a class to learn about driving safety and the different flags so he would be prepared to start driving. Roger had decided to take the car for a test drive just to make sure it was running smoothly. He went two laps around the track, and on the third lap as he was going straight at 140 mph his brakes and steering wheel locked up. The car wouldn't turn or slow down, and he slammed into the sidewall of the track at over 100 mph.

Roger told me later that when he hit the wall, the pain was so excruciating that he couldn't stay in the position that he was in. He can't remember if he opened the door or climbed out the window, but when people got to him he was lying on his back in the dirt, unable to move. All he remembers is just praying for Jesus to help him and save him. We are so thankful that he had his safety gear on—the harness saved his neck from breaking.

Zecharia was still in class when the accident happened, so they called his name over the loudspeaker to come to the paddock. His first thought was they just needed him to get to the track sooner. He said they kept calling his name over and over, and when he showed up and saw the ambulance he knew something was wrong. Roger had told the medics he didn't want to leave without seeing his son first.

Zech ended the call by letting me know they were taking Roger to the ICU for more testing, and he would call me again as soon as he had another update. It broke my heart thinking about my husband and son at the hospital without me, but I had no control. I had to give all my anxiety to the Lord and depend on Him completely.

Finally, the buses started leaving Myrtle Beach in the afternoon. Even though it was only hours since I had gotten the initial phone call from Zech, it felt like days had passed. My whole face felt dried up; I had cried all the tears I had in my body. I couldn't wait to get home and get to the hospital. By the time we got back to Priscilla's school, it was around 7 p.m. We went straight home, grabbed a few things for Roger and headed straight to the hospital. The ICU visiting hours closed at 8 p.m.—I don't think I've driven so fast in my life. Thankfully, we made it in time and Priscilla and I got to see him quickly before we had to leave.

It was so hard seeing my strong, tall, muscular husband lying in a bed covered in tubes and wires, so helpless. I remember one of the first things I asked him was if he could feel his feet; he said yes, but he couldn't move his body at all. I finally felt some relief in seeing him, touching him. He was alive. I remember also having the realization that I could have easily lost my husband and son that day; they were both supposed to be in that car driving together. I knew we had a long road ahead, but I was beyond grateful that he was still here with us.

As the kids and I left the ICU that night, I looked at my sixteen-year-old son and realized that he had become a man that day. He was so brave and had so much strength for his dad, me and his sister that day, never even shedding a tear as he stepped up to take care of his family. When we got home, I wrapped my arms around him and told him I was so proud of him, and thanked him for being so strong that day. Only then did he break down right there in my arms and finally let a flood of tears out. "I was so scared, Mom." To say it was a rough day for all of us would be an understatement.

First thing the next day, I returned to the hospital. Roger was in the ICU for four days, had back surgery and then spent two more days in the hospital. I spent most of each day with him, since he couldn't do anything on his own, not even eat. He wasn't supposed to move while they were working on his back. We finally got him home, and through weeks and months of rehab and physical therapy, he was able to walk again. It took one full year before he was back to functioning normally, the way he was before the accident.

Throughout his entire recovery process, we realized what an amazing village we had. I remember as soon as we pulled into our driveway the day we took Roger home, our neighbors Mr. Frank and Miss Jackie ran over as soon as they saw us to help me walk Roger into the house. They loaned us a power lift recliner, a portable toilet and other items that were lifesavers while Roger was recovering. His work family stepped up and took care of things while he was away, and our families and our church family were supportive as well. Even though it was such a difficult season, it was humbling to see how God had provided abundantly all and more that we needed.

It is all by God's grace that he is here and stronger than ever today. It was a rough road of recovery, but he was strong and determined. We have a small gym in our garage, and there were days he would try to crawl on the floor trying to regain his strength. Zech would also take him to the gym, help him get onto the machines and adjust all the weights for him. He had lost a considerable amount of weight being bedridden for months, so it took a lot of time and commitment for him to get his health back. Our kids were amazing through it all, helping each other and taking care of extra things to help us out. They were so brave, even pulling themselves together enough to go to school the Monday after the accident. Their relationships with the Lord carried them through this difficult time, enabling them to be as strong as they were. I get compliments on them all the time, people telling me what amazing children they are, but I know it's because of Jesus working in their hearts. In the end, it was only our family's faith in God that helped us endure this difficult trial.

Another thing that has helped grow my relationship with the Lord these past few years has been serving at our church with my family. It has been such a blessing for Roger and I to watch our children excel and choose to serve Jesus with their lives. I am so proud to be their mom—I know my sacrifices to stay home with them were not in vain. They are both honor roll students. Zech has two black belts in two different martial arts, while Priscilla is a wonderful piano player and singer. They both make Roger and I so proud.

The accident also made me even more thankful than I thought possible for the amazing, godly man that God gave me to do this life with as a partner. He works tirelessly to provide for his family and has always been an incredible father to our children. No life is perfect or without trouble, but coming where I came from I am so grateful for each day.

I learned that, at the end of the day, all I have is my faith. Roger has always been my rock, but I learned just how quickly he could be taken away. Things can change in the blink of an eye, and we have no control. His strength, our financial status, having our needs met and a million other things weren't what was going to get us through tough times. In a very real way, I learned that the only person I could rely on fully was my Father in heaven. Being a Christian doesn't make you immune to trauma or challenges in life, but it does give you the One you need to overcome them—Jesus. Our community of brothers and sisters in Christ were also invaluable as they rallied around us and supported us as we walked through that valley.

When Roger was still in the hospital recovering, I remember telling him how grateful I was that God had saved him and our son, but that I didn't want him driving on a racetrack ever again. We didn't talk about it again until he started to get his strength back, and he asked me about it. He still loved racing, and I didn't know what to say to him when he asked, because truthfully, I was terrified for him to ever race again.

He thought about selling all his equipment, and during the year he actually did sell one of his cars. I could see how badly he wanted to get back out there, so I told him to hold off on getting rid of anything else and that we could discuss it again when he was 100% healed. Once a year had passed and he was back to his normal self, I thought a lot about how racing was Roger's favorite hobby and how it brought him so much joy. I didn't want to be the one who stopped him from enjoying it again, but I was still so scared.

I prayed about it a lot, and God gave me a lot of peace in letting go and trusting Roger to Him. I realized he could easily have an accident anywhere, and I knew he took every safety precaution while on the track. I told him that I didn't feel right being the one to stop him from racing, and that it was his decision. Eventually, he did go back to racing and even won a few races. Zech still hasn't tried it yet, but has been thinking about doing it more recently. He and Roger share a love of racing; they even went to a Formula One race together in Belgium with my brother-in-law while we were visiting France the summer of 2024, which was an exciting experience for them to share together.

On the other side of the accident, I can see now how much God has used it for his glory. Even today, people stop me randomly and ask how Roger is doing, and I get to tell them about how he is a walking miracle. It has been an opportunity to plant gospel seeds in so many people, for which we are both so grateful. Our testimony for Christ becomes even stronger when we go through tough times and are able to praise our Savior through it all. The world is watching: how are we going to act and respond to trials as children of God?

That year, God continued to challenge me in this area. I still struggled with some health issues since my implant surgery;

much less than before, but one that kept popping up was pain in my lower abdomen. I went to my OBGYN and different specialists several times to try to figure out why I was having pain there, but no one had any answers. I was put on birth control pills for a while, which helped with some of the symptoms, but not all. By the time Roger had his accident and I was helping him recover, I was having serious pain on a regular basis that was keeping me up at night.

I remember during that year as Roger was going through rehab thinking, *Why God? Haven't we been through enough as a family? Haven't I been through enough? How many more health issues do I need?*

I was frustrated, which drove me to go back to the OBGYN in the fall that year to keep seeking answers. They did some different tests and found that I had a fibroid in my uterus the size of a golf ball, as well as polyps, cysts and scar tissue all over my abdomen, probably from my two c-sections. Basically, I was told that my abdomen was a warzone! The doctor recommended a total hysterectomy.

Of course, that was a scary diagnosis, especially while we were still dealing with Roger's recovery. We did a lot of praying and research before deciding to go ahead with the surgery. I remember thinking, *God, I have so many plans to serve you. Why do you keep throwing up roadblocks? Why is this happening? Do you not need me to do anything for you?*

On October 31st, 2023, I had the surgery. It was by far the most painful medical procedure I've ever endured. The surgery itself took over three hours, and afterwards I was in the hospital for two days. My surgeon told me, "No wonder you were in so much pain—you had a lot going on in there!" He told me some of my abdominal muscles had split, so they had to sew those up while they were in there, too.

My recovery has taken a long time—I'm still working on getting back to normal to this day. But while I was in bed recovering, I had a lot of time to spend with my Father and read His Word. It gave me time to reflect on my own life and on what is really important, and what my goals and mission should be. Lying there in bed, it became so clear to me—I wanted to continue serving the Lord. I wanted to be His disciple, His servant, His ambassador, and share His message all over the world. I realized how He had used all the pain and struggle from the past year to gently draw me even closer to Himself, and show me how He could use my brokenness for His glory.

It's time, Karima. It's time to write your story; now is your opportunity. Don't worry, I will supply you with everything you need. Just trust me. I still wrestled with feeling unqualified, uneducated, unimportant. *God, I'm just a girl from Morocco.*

We were still watching through "The Chosen" that year, and I found myself relating to so many women in the Bible. Like, for example, the bleeding woman in Luke 8:43-48. She suffered from a bleeding disease for twelve years and had spent all she had on doctors, but no one could cure her. She came up behind Jesus, touched the fringe of His robe and was healed immediately. Or, the Samaritan woman at the well in John 4:4-30. I related to how excited she was to tell everyone about Jesus. She had been rejected by everyone for years, but Jesus changed her heart and her story, and used her to reach her entire town with the gospel.

There was nothing special about these women. In fact, they were both outcasts who were going through their own difficult circumstances, and yet God used them to do His will. Maybe He can use me too. Okay, Lord. This is in Your hands.

In January 2024, I had lunch with my writer friend, Becky, and told her about my dream to write a book. Her first question was, "What are you going to call it?" I remembered my friend, Sarah, who came to my rescue when Roger was in his accident. Years ago, I had been talking to her about writing my book, and she had said, "Karima, when you write this, you should call it 'Muslim by Birth, Christian by Choice.'" I shared that story with Becky, and she thought it was a great name. I knew the Lord had ordained all of this through every interaction, every conversation, every trial. So, my book was born.

Roger and the kids have been my biggest cheerleaders, encouraging me long before I ever started writing. My other family and friends have also been so excited for me throughout this process; I've even talked to my family in Morocco, France and Spain about it, and all of them have been so supportive and helpful as I try to remember things from the past. They've helped me with so many stories I had forgotten, showed me things I used to do growing up and even sent old pictures of the family.

In the summer of 2024, Roger and the kids and I made another big trip out to France and Morocco to see all of my family. First, we went to France and saw my parents and sisters, who are now all grown up and married with their own children. My parents have had some of their own health challenges recently, so it was a sweet experience to see them and spend time with them. Then, we went to Morocco. Before our trip, we hadn't been back since 2015—it was the longest I had ever been away. We had been planning to go in 2020, but when COVID closed everything down it delayed us from being able to travel.

Together, we celebrated Zech's 18th birthday and my brother-in-law's 50th. My aunts and I planned a big party for them, with music and food and dancing, just like the old days. Everyone was so happy just spending time together; I'm so grateful the Lord allowed us to have that special moment all together.

One night, we all walked out to Jemaa el-Fnaa square, where everyone goes at night since it's so hot during the day. On the way back, one of my cousins and I were walking together and I was able to share my testimony with her on a deeper level, and she was receptive to what I was saying. I also had another opportunity while we were there to talk to her and her sister and share about the Lord again. Neither of them knew about what we had gone through with our grandmother; it's something none of us really talked about, so it was a blessing getting to share how God has worked in my life after my difficult childhood.

I realized during those conversations with my cousins how it can be especially difficult to share the gospel with a Muslim. In my opinion, it's easier to go to someone with no religious foundation and share the gospel than it is to share it with someone who has a strong religious background. To the first person, you are simply sharing your faith. But for the second, you are also having to explain why what they are believing in is not true. This concept took me so long to grasp for myself, and I only grew up entrenched in Islam for twelve years.

The best treat of all, though, happened one random morning while we were there. My aunt who I used to beg with all the time needed to run out and get something from the market, and I offered to go with her. As we started walking, I realized that I hadn't been out in the souk with her since we used to beg together as little girls, almost 40 years ago.

As we walked those familiar winding streets, the memories all flooded back—the early pitch black mornings, the kicks to wake us up, the smell of freshly baked pastries. It was a surreal moment. Tears came to my eyes as we talked and laughed, reminiscing about all the time we spent in that souk together. I was filled with an overwhelming sense of gratitude that God would allow me to have that moment, to reflect on how far I had come from that scared, little Moroccan girl to the confident woman of faith I was now.

The last night we were there, we were all gathered together in the center of my grandmother's house, and one of my aunts got up and shared how thankful she was that Roger and I had helped them out financially during COVID. She said she was speaking for the whole family in expressing their gratitude for us. Roger got up and told them, "You are all our family. We will always be here for you to help you."

As I sat with my family watching this scene unfold, tears escaped my eyes as I realized yet again how much God had provided for me, and how grateful I was that God could use me to help my family now.

Roger and the kids and I pray daily for my extended family, that they would find the truth of Jesus for themselves, and discover all the love and hope He has to offer. I know my job isn't to save anyone; my mission is to simply plant seeds, like Paul explains in 1 Corinthians 3:5-9:

> *What then is Apollos? What is Paul? Servants through whom you believed, as the Lord assigned to each. I planted,*

Apollos watered, but God gave the growth. So neither he who plants nor he who waters is anything, but only God who gives the growth. He who plants and he who waters are one, and each will receive his wages according to his labor. For we are God's fellow workers. You are God's field, God's building. (ESV)

I've seen this over and over again in my own life, looking back at all the people who planted seeds in me and never knew the impact they had. Then, Roger watered, and God grew, and here I am today. I am a living testimony that growth doesn't happen overnight, and there may be some cases where we never see it in someone we are praying for; but we can't allow that to discourage us. If we never try to share the good news of the gospel, then how will anyone hear it? Christians must go out into the world and into uncomfortable situations and be bold, unafraid, like the Bible says in Joshua 1:9: "Have I not commanded you? Be strong and courageous. Do not be frightened, and do not be dismayed, for the Lord your God is with you wherever you go." (ESV) I am thankful for those who boldly shared with me and that God didn't give up on me, or I wouldn't be here today.

God never gives up on His people, and He can use even the most broken, the most helpless and the most needy for His glory. So never say never; I am a living example of the bold declaration in Matthew 19:26, "With God, all things are possible."

Therefore, since we are surrounded by such a great cloud of witnesses, let us throw off everything that hinders and the sin that so easily entangles. And let us run with perseverance the race marked out for us, fixing our eyes on Jesus, the pioneer and perfecter of faith. For the joy set before him he endured the cross, scorning its shame, and sat down at the right hand of the throne of God. Hebrews 12:1-2.

Roger as Superman proposing to me on top of the Savannah globe in April of 2001.

My Superman

God's mercy on display; I am standing in the souk of Marrakech, where I used to beg tourists for money, with the American man of my dreams.

Our wedding ceremony in Morocco

Our big, formal wedding in 2002

Morocco 2024. Here I have henna on my hands, as we were preparing to enjoy a small celebration at my grandmother's house.

Morocco 2024, at my grandmother's house eating soup and dates for breakfast with the family.

Visiting my second school from childhood; it was still open in 2024.

Dressed up for the family celebration

Invitation

If this book impacted you and you want to trust Jesus as your personal Savior, or if you have questions about your faith, please go out and buy a Bible today. Don't believe my words—believe God's Word. Then, go find a Bible-believing local church, and get involved with a Christian community.

To accept Jesus as your Savior, the Bible says it is very simple. Romans 10:13 says that "everyone who calls on the name of the Lord will be saved." Bow your head, close your eyes and just talk to your Creator. He loves you so much, and is willing and waiting to bring you into His family. Here is a short prayer guide if you are struggling with what to pray.

> *Father God, I want to be your child. I know that I am a sinner in need of a Savior. I believe that you sent your Son, Jesus, down to this earth to die on the cross for my sins. I believe that He rose from the dead and is now in heaven with you. Please forgive me for everything I've done wrong and wash me white as snow. Please come live in my heart and change me. I want to live my life for you. Thank you for loving me and accepting me as Your child. In Jesus' name, Amen.*

About the Author

Karima Burdette is a Christian YouTuber, social media influencer, motivational speaker and author. She has been married to her husband, Roger, for 24 years, and they have four children and five grandchildren. Driven by her desire to serve the Lord and others, she is an active member of her local church, and her favorite things to do are spend time with her family, serve her community and tell people about Jesus. Her life's motto is that "even the smallest act of kindness can give hope to those who have none."

Endnote Review Request

If you enjoyed reading this, please leave a review on Amazon. I read every review and they help new readers discover my books.

—Karima Burdette

To learn more about Karima Burdette's ministry, subscribe to @lifechatwithkarima on YouTube.

For bookings, please go to https://karimaburdette.com.

Notes

Notes

Notes

Notes

Notes

Made in the USA
Columbia, SC
15 May 2025